Sociology for GCSE and Beyond

David Spurling

authorHOUSE

AuthorHouse™ UK
1663 Liberty Drive
Bloomington, IN 47403 USA
www.authorhouse.co.uk
Phone: 0800.197.4150

© 2017 David Spurling. All rights reserved.

No part of this book may be reproduced, stored in a retrieval system, or transmitted by any means without the written permission of the author.

Published by AuthorHouse   12/13/2016

ISBN: 978-1-5246-6666-8 (sc)
ISBN: 978-1-5246-6667-5 (e)

The author wishes to thank Poppy Cole, Tim Westby and Lois Wakefield for their help preparing this book.

Print information available on the last page.

Any people depicted in stock imagery provided by Thinkstock are models, and such images are being used for illustrative purposes only. Certain stock imagery © Thinkstock.

This book is printed on acid-free paper.

Because of the dynamic nature of the Internet, any web addresses or links contained in this book may have changed since publication and may no longer be valid. The views expressed in this work are solely those of the author and do not necessarily reflect the views of the publisher, and the publisher hereby disclaims any responsibility for them.

Contents

Chapter 1	Studying Society	1
Chapter 2	Research Methods	3
Chapter 3	Education	14
Chapter 4	Ethnicity	24
Chapter 5	Gender	30
Chapter 6	Family	46
Chapter 7	Social class and mobility	67
Chapter 8	Changing patterns of work	76
Chapter 9	Mass media	81
Chapter 10	Politics and voting behaviour	94
Chapter 11	Socialisation and culture	98
Chapter 12	Poverty and the welfare state	106
Chapter 13	Modernisation theory	111
Chapter 14	Religion	120
Chapter 15	Crime and deviance	130
Chapter 16	Climate Change, the environment and Global Warming	153
Chapter 17	Globalisation	167
Chapter 18	Typical exam questions	194
Chapter 19	Glossary of terms	207
Chapter 20	How to use this book to get the best possible marks in GCSE sociology or equivalent exams	242
Chapter 21	Index	245
Chapter 22	Bibliography	248

Chapter 1 — Studying Society

Defining Sociology

Sociology can be defined as the study of society. A society can be defined as a group of individuals who share a culture, norms, values or a way of life. This can alternatively be known as a community. It can be described more formally as the study of the development, structure and function of human society. Sociology is unlike some other sciences, such as mathematics, where a series of propositions will usually lead to definite conclusions. It differs from biology since we can often experiment with plants to improve the yield or in some cases to try to suppress plants such as Japanese knotweed, which causes many problems in the UK. We cannot often carry out experiments in sociology without informed consent.

Sociology is often defined as a social science because it deals with the ways in which human beings interact with each other. It looks at the ways in which people make decisions about other people and why they interact in that way. In society, there is often room for disagreement, because of differences and unpredictability in the ideas and behaviour of individuals.

Introduction to social theories and institutions

Functionalism (a consensus theory), Marxism and feminism (conflict theories) are the main three structured theories within sociology. Functionalists see society as being beneficial for every institution but are often criticised by other theories for ignoring the conflict in society. Marxists see only the conflict between classes, claiming we live in a capitalist society and ignore other conflicts such as gender, while feminists only see the conflicts between gender, claiming we live in a patriarchal society and ignore other conflicts such as class and race.

A patriarchal society means a society where men make the majority of decisions, and have a much better lifestyle than women. Consensus assumes that the majority of people within a society are trying to find ways to live together harmoniously. Conflict means where one group is trying to dominate another group.

The main institutions that make up society are the family, the Education System, the Criminal Justice System and the social stratification system. Each theory explores the social processes and social issues that belong to each institution.

Self-assessment questions

Q1. In what ways is sociology different and in what ways is it similar to the physical sciences?

Q2. Why does the unpredictability of human behaviour make it more difficult to test ideas than in the study of physics or mathematics?

Q3. Some people have suggested that we can learn from animal behaviour about human behaviour. How far is this true and why it is important?

Q4. What are the main theories of human behaviour within sociology?

Q5. What is meant by the phrase, sociology is a social science?

Q6. What are the main institutions in UK society? In what ways are they similar to other societies such as the USA or India or China and in what ways are they different?

Chapter 2   Research Methods

Carrying out sociological research

Social theories often disagree with each other not only because their views are biased, but also because they have inadequate data to use in investigations. In many cases, it is important to look at both primary and secondary data. The term "secondary data" refers to information that has been used and collected for other purposes, for instance, information from government surveys.

Primary and secondary data

Primary data means data that organisations collect for their own purpose. While primary data would fully serve the purpose of intended research, it is expensive to obtain, unlike secondary data, which is often cheaper and more readily accessible.

Formulating hypotheses

Sociologists can carry out their research in many different ways. Before starting any study, it is important to identify and develop research aims and hypotheses. This means researchers need to know exactly what they intend to investigate and what their informed opinion of the outcome is.

Pilot studies

Once a researcher has these, they can then create a pilot study. This is like a mini trial run of the research before the main study takes place and has the purpose of identifying any problems or changes that need to be made to make the study more reliable and effective.

Pilot studies may help to eliminate any embarrassing questions if rewording led to less embarrassment. They may also discover that the range of options given to interviewees does not cover the entire range of potential answers. For example, transport questionnaires do not always mention the possibility of using ferry services even when this is an option.

Once the pilot study is complete, the researcher may then select a sample from the following categories: random sampling, stratified sampling, snowball sampling and systematic sampling. Sampling saves time, money and resources.

Often pilot studies will show that people may be embarrassed about their family, income or disclosing their age. Sometimes people do not actually know their age. (Some, particularly the elderly, will say, "I am in my 77th year." rather than saying they are 76.) The NHS carries out health checks on older people to check for dementia. They also give what are called MOT tests to a selection of people over 40.

Current statistics show that the NHS knows that people waste prescriptions. There is no method of checking between the pharmacies and the medical practitioners about what is happening.

Apart from embarrassment, people often do not know how much their spouse earns; this makes it difficult to gauge the effects of different measures central or local government may take.

Pilot studies also help people to realise they know little about safe limits for alcohol. Nor do they have a real understanding of the concept of a standard unit of alcohol.

Pilot studies may also show that the effects of drugs are little understood whether these are prescribed drugs, bought over-the-counter drugs, or illegal drugs.

Lack of knowledge by people filling in questionnaires

In education, students completing year 11 have not always been informed about the possibility of taking an apprenticeship even though the government wishes more people to take up apprenticeships, particularly in engineering.

People may be reluctant to admit that they have not heard of particular books or watched particular TV programmes, and may try to impress the interviewer, particularly if they are attracted to the interviewer.

People may also want to boast about, or understate, the number of people they have had sex with, so figures are unreliable.

Sometimes travel firms will ask about the number of journeys they have made in the past year, and, unless those journeys were particularly memorable, it seems unlikely the figures will be accurate.

The number of times that people will have been to a particular shopping centre, or even a particular shop, is likely to be an inaccurate estimate.

It would be difficult for to give estimates about what would be for them completely new goods or services. For example, before the Channel Tunnel opened in 1994, the original estimate was for 20 million passengers a year, whereas the actual usage was around 7 to 8 million a year.

Similarly, asking businesses about what happens after Brexit.

Obtaining information about illegal immigration is, by definition, difficult, as we have no way of knowing how many illegal immigrants there are in any country. Comments from the right-wing media about the lack of infrastructure and problems of the NHS seem odd, as one estimate is that around 70% of doctors below the rank of consultant are from overseas.

Random sampling

This is when every member of the population has an equal chance of being selected for the research.

We can often obtain our sampling frame from the electoral register in the UK, which should list all the people over 18 years eligible to vote. This will include all British citizens, European Union citizens for some elections, as well as Irish citizens. However, not all people, especially the young, are on the election register, so we cannot be sure that we will get a random sample. This could be important for some items such as the number of people going to clubs, but might be less important for the number of people requiring hearing aids.

When looking at the number of people watching the Eurovision song contest, it might be difficult to have a random sample, since there is no obvious method of getting a sample across the UK.

On the other hand, if we wanted to have a survey of junior doctors in 2016 this would be easier to obtain from the relevant authorities and could be vital if we wanted to gauge their reactions to the latest pay and conditions offer from the government.

Stratified sampling

Stratified sampling occurs where the researcher separates the population into sub groups according to certain characteristics such as gender, age, income, ethnicity and religion. The researcher will then randomly select a sample from each of these groups, keeping the numbers in proportion with the population.

If we were to investigate borrowing from college or school libraries, then we might want to use stratified sampling. We might wish to see how many people borrowed sociology books, how many borrowed mathematics books, how many borrowed books on English literature or drama, etc. This would be particularly important if there are likely to be budget cuts in the library system.

Currently, many local authorities are cutting down on public library expenditure.

Snowball sampling

This is when a sample occurs through contacts when one member of the population introduces the researcher to another member, and so on.

Realistically, this may be the only way to get in touch with people where there is not an association or other data from which to interview people. This could apply, for example, to people who like a particular type of music, such as garage, grunge, or Gregorian chant, where there is no reason why there should be a central register of such people. This will be in contrast to the people attending BBC promenade concerts at the Albert Hall.

Snowball sampling is also used by organisations wanting to persuade people to invest in social ventures where profit is not the main aim.

Similarly, firms selling solar panels or heat extractors will often ask their customers if they can provide names of other people who might be interested in having these installed. There is virtually no other way for the organisation to this.

Business organisations might also use this to sell the latest telephone and broadband packages.

Schools and colleges might use similar techniques to sell tickets for dramatic productions, concerts, or other events.

Systematic sampling

This is when the researcher decides on a number (n) and takes every n^{th} item from the sampling frame.

Once the sample has been selected, the research can then be carried out in order for the researcher to collect their data. The researcher might like to use primary methods such as surveys, observation or interviews. However, they may also like the aid of secondary data to back up their primary findings, such as the use of official statistics.

Once the data has been collected, it must be analysed in order to interpret and make sense of the findings.

The last step in any research study is to evaluate the study's aims, methods and findings. This can be done by identifying and evaluating the practicality, ethical issues, reliability, validity, effectiveness, representation and the theory.

Practical issues

Before carrying out a study the researcher should be aware of how long their study will take, and what effect that will have on the cost. In longitudinal studies, we look at the same group of people over a long period. By definition, this will take a lot longer than most other methods and will therefore be costly. The researcher must also consider how they are going to gain access to the group they are studying, as it is not always easy to be accepted into a new group, whether the experiment is overt or covert. Overt means we are open about what we are doing, and covert means we hide the objectives of our research.

Ethical issues

Ethical issues are very likely to occur in sociological experiments. First of all, the researcher must gain consent from the participants and, in the cases of working with minors, they must gain parental consent. It can take a long time to gain such consent, therefore costing the researcher more. The consent the participants give must be informed so that the participants can decide how much information they want to share with the researcher.

Another issue to consider is confidentiality. The information the researcher receives must be confidential and anonymous. This can sometimes hinder the effectiveness of the research, as some findings may be unusable. As well as this, the researcher is at risk of being exposed to guilty knowledge, especially when investigating a sensitive subject. Alongside this, the researcher could be put at risk of physical and psychological harm, especially when undercover. With covert operations, there is always the danger of being found out, and especially when investigating a group such as a gang, the consequences could be life threatening. Similarly, the actions the researcher may witness could cause psychological harm if they are exposed to violent or immoral acts. Again, there is also the risk of the researcher going native, as to fit in with a group and disguising their true intentions could cause them to participate with the behaviour of that group, therefore hindering the validity and reliability of the research.

Participants must always be offered the right to withdraw and their decision should be respected. This can put a gap in the findings, as well as decreasing the sample size, causing an unrepresentative sample.

Many concerns are raised by ordinary people about the confidentiality of the information they give. In particular, there have been concerns about the Investigatory Powers Bill, referred to as the "Snoopers' Charter" by people worrying that the government can listen in to any phone conversations, read everybody's emails, scrutinise all online activity, and even hack into any computer or electronic device.

There have also been concerns that confidential information is sold on to commercial organisations when it clearly should not be.

The electoral register which local authorities have to produce, are not meant to be used for commercial purposes, but organisations often use them.

The media often suggest that they have a right to look for information even if the government does not want them to do so, and there have been discussions about what constitutes public interest. It is difficult to see how hacking into a murdered schoolgirl's phone messages (Millie Dowler) could be regarded as in the public interest.

Reliability issues

Many studies are hard to replicate, as the findings would be different in different places and with different individuals. This is particularly true for observational studies, as people are not always put into the exact same situation and circumstance and external factors can influence behaviour. When questionnaires and interviews are unstructured, the study is then hard to replicate: the method is made individual to each participant because of qualitative data.

Validity issues

Many factors can affect the validity of an experiment, especially its location. This is because the information obtained from participants is likely to be truer and of higher validity if the experiment is carried out in their natural setting. This is because the participants will seem more relaxed and at ease compared to being in a lab, therefore they are likely to display their usual behaviour. Unstructured methods and observations are likely to be more valid as the information obtained would be more detailed and in depth in comparison to a method such as official statistics. If an overt study is, being carried out the participants may not act as naturally as they would if they did not know they were being observed. Because of this the Halo Effect and Hawthorne Effect could occur, therefore causing the validity of the experiment to decrease.

The Halo effect is where if people [A] expect someone else [B] to behave well then they [A? B?] will probably do so [too?] whereas if we [A?] expect someone [B?] to do badly then they [B?] will probably behave in a bad way.

The Hawthorne experiment indicated that management taking an interest in workers and their conditions improved productivity almost irrespective of what the managers did.

Representativeness issues

Sociologists will wish to apply results from an experiment. However, these findings cannot be applied to the whole of society if the experiment was carried out on a much smaller scale. It would be wise to increase the sample size in order to increase the representativeness of a study and include people from different social groups and locations. If all the participants are of the same age group, the same sex and the same location, the results would not necessarily apply to the whole of society as such a group would not be representative of the whole population.

Qualitative and Quantitative Methods

When choosing a research method, it is important to know whether the data that will be obtained will be qualitative or quantitative. Qualitative data is more in depth, and is presented in a verbal or visual form. Examples of secondary qualitative data include written documents, such as newspaper clippings and diary entries, while primary qualitative methods include unstructured interviews and observations.

Quantitative data is presented in a statistical or numerical form and is often favoured by scientists. An example of quantitative data is official statistics. In the United Kingdom, a good deal of information can be obtained free of charge from the Office for National Statistics. The document "Measuring National Well-being", formerly called "Social Trends", is particularly helpful to the Sociologist.

Example of research methods

A report from three British universities, reported in the Guardian 20th April 2016,[1] concluded that the number of new cases of dementia in the UK was around 210,000 whereas it had been expected to be around 250,000.

It was important because it suggests that preventative action, which includes stopping smoking or reducing cholesterol, can reduce the risks of getting dementia. The research from the universities of Cambridge, East Anglia, and Newcastle had originally looked at 10,000 adults over 65 in the period between 1990 and 1995 and had subsequently carried out a second study between 2008 in 2013. Dementia rates have fallen by around 20% in that period in the period in the 1990s, 12.9% men out of every thousand went on to develop dementia, whereas this is now just 8.7 per thousand. However, perhaps surprisingly, women between 80 and 84 showed an increase in rates of dementia, which was reported in the same article.

An article by Ben Quinn[2] suggested that loneliness increased the risks of both strokes and heart attacks. The research was carried out by people from universities of York, Liverpool and Newcastle. It is suggested that loneliness and isolation increased the risk by around

30%. However, there may be other factors involved, according to the British Heart Foundation, since it is suggested that loneliness and having few social contacts can lead to more smoking, which in itself will lead to higher numbers of deaths.

A report by Alan Travis[3] suggested that that the response from 91 accident and emergency departments, minor injury units and walk-in centres showed that 210,000 people needed treatment, having been violently attacked in the 12 months up to September 2015. The research from Cardiff University suggested that the first time in seven years, there was a slight increase in the number of incidents reported.

The effect of junior doctors' strikes was analysed by Stephen Fabes, a junior doctor.[4] He stated that strikes would protect patients, rather than hurting them. 98% of junior doctors were striking in April 2016. There are problems for the NHS since many doctors wish to leave within a short period, even though their training costs to the NHS are very expensive.

Around 45,000 medics below the rank of consultant took part in the strikes in April 2016. The General Medical Council suggested that lives could be lost because of the complete strike action, which was the first one ever in NHS history.

Some newspapers such as the Guardian have a good reputation for using accurate, useful data. Other newspapers such as the Sun have a very poor reputation, especially after the Hillsborough disaster 1989. This disaster killed 96 Liverpool fans. The original newspaper report suggested that it was the fans' fault. In April 2016, after a long inquest, it was shown that the police had lied at the time, and the idea that the fans had attacked the police and other people trying to help the players was completely erroneous.

Self-examination questions

Q1. What are the different social factors that affect human behaviour and society? Why might it be difficult to get agreement on how important these different influences are?

Q2. Why is it important to check that any data we have is as unbiased as possible? How can sociologists help to ensure that data we have is representative?

Q3. What is meant by a pilot study? Why might pilot studies mean that we can avoid embarrassing questions being asked unless strictly necessary?

Q4. What different sampling methods can be used? What are their respective advantages and disadvantages?

Q5. A sociology course should help you to appreciate different ways of living in a society such as the United Kingdom. How can it help you to do this?

Q6. What are the advantages and disadvantages of using local newspapers as a source of information?

Q7. What are the advantages and disadvantages of using national newspapers as a source of information? Give examples to support your opinion.

Q8. Why is it important to be able to obtain representative samples in sociology?

---

1   Nicola Davis, "Drop in dementia rates suggests disease can be prevented, researchers say", The Guardian, 19th April 2016, http://gu.com/p/4teqz
2   Ben Quinn, "Loneliness linked to 30% increase in heart disease and stroke risk", The Guardian, 19th April 2016, http://gu.com/p/4tf64
3   Alan Travis, "Decline in violent crime ends as attacks against older people rise", The Guardian, 20th April 2016, http://gu.com/p/4tfvt
4   Stephen Fabes, "Harm patients? Junior doctors are striking to protect them", The Guardian, 19th April 2016, http://gu.com/p/4tf26

Chapter 3 — Education

Education is one form of secondary socialisation and can be split into two categories: formal and informal. Formal education takes place in educational institutions such as schools, colleges and universities, whereas informal education takes place by individuals observing the actions of others around them.

Types of Education

The education system in the United Kingdom includes several stages.

Preschool/early year's education

This type of education is provided for 3-4 year olds to prepare them for school life. In 2016, the government wanted new nursery assistants to have at least a good GCSE in English and maths. The providers, however, thought that empathy was much more important than a formal qualification. In some other countries, compulsory education does not start until later on in life. This is partly because it is assumed that education will take place within the family rather than in school.

Primary education

This type of education is aimed at students aged 5-11. However, there is also *middle schools*, and although these are now less common, they cater for students from 9 to the age of 13.

Secondary education

Students stay in education between the ages of 11-18, but can choose which type of secondary school they would like to go to, dependent on their abilities. Academies, specialist, faith, comprehensive and grammar schools and public schools are all types of secondary education.

Further education

Further education used to be optional but due to a change in law, students must stay at school until they are 18. This type of education can be obtained in sixth forms and further education colleges.

Higher education

This sector refers to university degree-level studies and also professional examinations.

The Role of Formal Education

Functionalist View

Functionalists focus on and identify the positive role of education, while ignoring the conflict that can occur within the institution. They claim that the main purposes of the educational system are:

To serve the needs of the economy

This means that the educational system prepares individuals with the correct knowledge and skills needed to become a future worker to benefit their country in a competitive global economy.

Secondary socialisation

While attending school, students are able to learn more about their society by exploring the norms and values of their culture.

Social Control

The educational system uses socialisation from the family by teaching students to conform to school rules and have respect for older generations. This is enforced through positive, negative, informal and formal sanctions.

Selection

The education system is often compared to a sieve as it filters students by their grades, which then allows them into certain jobs dependent on their individual abilities and results.

Enabling social mobility

The educational system gives students an opportunity to move up (or down) the social ladder. This means that even if a student is from a disadvantaged background where they may suffer from material and/or cultural deprivation they still have the chance to excel in school and move up the social class system. Theresa May the new Conservative Prime Minister surprised many people in 2016 by stating that new grammar schools would be built to help social mobility.

Encouraging social cohesion and 'Britishness'

Formal education in the UK allows students to identify and explore the British culture by seeing themselves as British citizens. This helps to increase and reinforce social cohesion and allows society to unite as a whole, regardless of sub groups such as age and gender.

Currently there is a great deal of discussion about how far education can help to counter radical Muslim ideas. However, less attention has been paid to counter the extreme-right factions that have resulted in violence towards people of different ethnic and religious groups especially following Brexit.

Although Functionalists help point out the positive impacts the education system has on society, they often ignore other conflict within society and are therefore often criticised by other theorists.

Marxist View

Marxists use a different approach and claim that the role of the education system is to:

Provide secondary socialisation

This is a point that both Marxists and Functionalists agree on. However, Marxists take the view that the education system forces working class children to accept their lower rank in capitalist society. This is by learning to accept the hierarchy and to obey rules or face sanctions.

Reproduce the class system

Although the education system appears to reward all students equally based upon their individual abilities, Marxists claim that this is untrue. They believe that it favours students from more advantaged backgrounds as these students will have access to resources that materially deprived students will not. This means that the higher-class students have more opportunities to do well and will then get better-paid jobs than working class children who do not have access to the same means.

Breed competition

Competition brews in all schools, not just in actual sport or music competitions but also in exam results. Therefore, the education system stresses the value of competition and Marxists claim that the capitalist system is also based on competition.

Serve the interests of the ruling class

Education passes on ideas and beliefs that support the idea that the capitalist society is meritocratic and fair, even though Marxists claim that it is not.

Marxists, therefore, state always why the education system works in a capitalist society but they do ignore the fact that this does not always apply. There have been cases where social mobility has indeed occurred for some students, thus reducing social class reproduction.

Educational Achievement
Class

According to official statistics, students from a middle-class background achieve better examination results than those from a working-class background.

Arguments why this is so include:

- Members of the working class by definition do not have the same funds as members of the middle class and upper class and therefore are likely to suffer from material deprivation. Therefore, the upper classes have access to material that the working class cannot afford and therefore have an advantage when studying. These materials can include textbooks, stationery, personal tutor etc.

- Due to norms and values passed down in families, members of the working class often do not value education highly and therefore do not encourage their children to do well. This is known as cultural deprivation as these students would be at a disadvantage compared to those who are encouraged and motivated to achieve highly in education. Parents of upper class children often have more input and interest into their child's education, whereas working class families value different things.

- The labelling theory suggests that as working class students do not follow the same norms and values as upper class students, they are likely to be labelled within the education system as being unintelligent and disruptive. This label can come about from working class children simply not having enough money for the correct school uniform. As the student, would then look scruffy in comparison to the upper class well-presented students, the teacher may then give them a negative label. Working-class students may not achieve as highly in their homework as upper class students as they do not have access to the right materials at home and again this can add to the illusion that these students do not work hard. This negative label can then have a negative impact upon a student as their hard work does not their teachers' expectations of them and so a self- fulfilling prophecy can occur. This is when the student lives up to their negative label and becomes disruptive and stops working hard as they feel they have little chance of achievement.

Discipline in schools

In the United Kingdom, corporal punishment has been abolished. Sociologists belonging to the New Right school of thought will probably assume that this is why there has been a lack of discipline in schools. UK surveys have shown that, perhaps unsurprisingly, the vast majority of parents think that teachers should be allowed to be tougher when it comes to discipline. Perhaps more surprisingly the majority of students also agree, but by a much smaller margin, that discipline should be tougher. Some sociologists have suggested that the absence of a male role model both within the family and within primary schools does not help.

OFSTED assesses the behaviour of pupils at schools as one of its four criteria; the others are the standard of teaching, the standard of schools' leadership and the achievement of pupils.

Education and budget cuts in 2016

Head teachers' leaders have warned secondary schools to consider axing subjects that few pupils take to cope with imminent budget cuts.

The Association of School and College Leaders told the Times Educational Supplement that A-levels in foreign languages, for example, could be scrapped. French dropped out of the top 10 most popular GCSEs for the first time.[5] "Languages in some schools will be vulnerable," he said. "We are already worried about them and this could speed up the decline."

The gender gap and education

The 2015 A-level results showed as before the difference between genders in popularity between subjects was very acute in some subjects. For example, only 8.5% of people taking computing were girls. Physics had only 21% female entrants. Further mathematics had only 28% female entrants. In contrast, 77% of sociology students were girls. 76% of psychology students, 72% of English students and 69% of drama students were female.

The Institute of Physics has carried out research about gender stereotyping and unsurprisingly wants teachers' and students' stereotyping to be challenged.

Size of schools and educational establishments

Whilst parents often like the idea of small village schools where teachers will often know the students and their families very well, some other sociologists have suggested that mega schools where a wide variety of subjects can be studied is very helpful. This will be even more crucial as students have to stay in education until the age of 18. Mega schools will have the usual advantages of economies of scale i.e. they can afford better computer and science equipment. They can also have specialist rooms for drama and music. There can also be a greater number of clubs whether for sporting or academic purposes and this can be helpful to overcome any problems of loneliness. Such clubs can also provide social cohesion.

Information from novels and films

"Tom Brown's Schooldays"[6] is a Victorian novel, published in 1857, that highlights the bullying at a public school (Rugby). The author Thomas Hughes had been a student at the school (1834 to 1842) so the work reflected his experiences at that time. It is worthwhile reading or watching a film version, since it helps to understand the educational problems at that time for the middle and upper class in a boarding school. Similarly, "Goodbye Mr Chips"[7] highlights the tensions in the First World War when a German teacher is faced with English students in a public school. The original book is based on the experience of that period and whilst sentimental gives an indication of education in that period.

Self-examination questions

Q1. Why are sociologists interested in the relationship between social class and educational performance?

Q2. Why might it be helpful to have a longitudinal study of students going through the same educational examinations, but at different schools? What problems might there be in trying to do this?

Q3. Why have sociologists looked at different types of educational provision and how it affects educational performance?

Q4. In the United Kingdom, public schools have often prided themselves on their small classes. Why might there be a relationship between size of class and educational performance? If there is a relationship, should this affect education in the state schools and academies?

Q5. The government has often published league tables about different types of schools. What problems can there be in interpreting the results of these tables?

Q6. Why might the amount of effort that students use have an effect on educational performance? Why might it be difficult to measure this effort?

Q7. Why might student's behaviour in class have an impact upon other students' educational performance?

Q8. Some students have a reputation for being sink schools. This means that parents and students who have a choice will not want to go to them. Why might it be difficult for poorer parents and students to be able to avoid going to these schools?

Q9. What difference will the raising of the school leaving age to 18 make to schools?

Q10. In March 2016, a survey of teachers in England and Wales stated that half of them wished to leave the service in the next five years. Will all of them be able to achieve this objective, and if so what difference would it make to the educational system?

Q11. In 2016, the government announced that it would wish all existing schools to become Academies. It later backtracked on this after opposition from the teaching unions as well as from some Conservative MPs. Academies do not have to appoint teachers with teaching qualifications. How might this affect their educational performances?

Q12. What is meant by informal education and why might it be very important for some students? Why might the type of family structure affect the amount of informal education that students receive?

Q13. Some sociologists have suggested that mega schools have advantages, since students can be offered a wider variety of subjects and experience than in small schools. Others suggest, however, that small schools, where parents and teachers may know each other, can be helpful. In what ways, can different research methods help to determine which type of school is most helpful.

Q14. What is meant by formal and informal education? Why are social scientists, including sociologists interested in both?

Q15. Different societies have different views about when children should start school and what qualifications nursery helpers need. Can sociologists help to determine the optimum age at which children should begin formal education?

Q16. What views do functionalists hold about education?

Q17. How does good schooling help to provide social mobility and why might this be important?

Q18. Which sociologists would hold the views that competition between schools and colleges is extremely helpful? Which sociologists would suggest that it is not?

Q19. What alternatives are there to going to university? What are the advantages and disadvantages of the alternatives?

Q20. What is meant by labelling theory? Why is it important?

Q21. Why might knowledge of foreign languages be important in the future for Britain's economic performance?

---

5   Jeevan Vasagar and Jessica Shepherd, "GCSE results: Pupils spurn languages for sciences", The Guardian, 24th August 2010, https://gu.com/p/2j8xn
6   Thomas Hughes, "Tom Brown's School Days", Macmillan, 1857, ISBN 978-0-19-283535-2
7   James Hilton, "Goodbye, Mr. Chips", Hodder & Stoughton, London, 1934

Chapter 4   Ethnicity

Sociologists usually use the word ethnicity rather than race.

Racism has often been a problem, as was clearly seen during the Nazi era in Germany in 1933 onwards when around 6 million Jews were killed in concentration camps along with other groups such as homosexuals and gypsies.

The term ethnic cleansing was used in the 1980s particularly with the killings in Bosnia. Later in 2016, one of the Bosnian leaders, Radovan Karadžić, was convicted of crimes against humanity.

Racism was also prevalent in Rwanda during the Civil War 1990- 1993 when life expectancy fell to around 20 for the typical Rwandan citizen.

Eugenics

Partly because of the domination of much of the world in the 19th century by people of European descent, there was interest in a pseudo-science called eugenics. This allegedly showed that there was a link between brain size and different races. Sir Francis Galton, a relative of Charles Darwin, who is best known for his theories on evolution, was particularly interested in this concept. There is very little link between brain size and intelligence, anyway. Partly because of his link with Darwin, eugenics has sometimes been described as social Darwinism. Eugenics was accepted by many people directly or indirectly during the interwar period 1918 to 39.

Whilst racists have often suggested that we do not have enough social infrastructure such as schools and hospitals to cope with more immigration, it has also been estimated that around 70% of doctors below the rank of consultant are from minority ethnic groups.

Race as a scapegoat

Hitler blamed the Jews for having helped Germany lose the First World War, even though many Jews had fought on the German side. A plausible hypothesis is that a puritan group, who work hard and plough money back into the business rather than spending money on luxuries, are likely to do well. This would be in line with Weber's Protestant work ethic.[8] A successful group are likely to arouse envy from other groups who do not wish to work hard.

Immigration and poor housing conditions

Successive groups of poor immigrants have often come to the inner-city areas, mainly because prices of houses have been cheaper, there than in the suburbs.

There are different patterns of immigration and housing, partly because even in one area, such as Bradford, the Indians often come from a more liberal wealthy background than the Pakistani's who often come from poorer parts of Pakistan.

The pattern will also depend upon the financial institutions and who they choose to lend money to and where.

Asylum seekers

Whilst the right-wing press often uses this term as a form of abuse, anyone who uses their knowledge of current events can see the horrors many people face when living in countries such as Syria, Libya, and Iraq, especially with the rise of so-called Islamic state.

Assimilation

Some people have suggested that people entering the UK permanently should have a good knowledge of the British culture, although it is not always clear what is meant by this.

Multiculturalism

There have been demonstrations, sometimes violent against multiculturalism as in Dover in April 2016. In practice, culture has many different layers for example, people from India and Pakistan and the West Indies will often enjoy cricket, whereas other ethnic groups will not. Similarly, different types of music such as the gospel-based singers including the late Dusty Springfield and even Elvis Presley may appeal, to a number of different groups, whatever their own personal background.

In the USA Pres Donald Trump's unexpected presidential election victory was attributed by some sociologists to anti-multiculturalism.

Ethnicity and education

According to official statistics, Chinese students perform better in examinations than any other ethnic group, whereas Afro Caribbean students tend to receive the lowest marks.

Arguments to explain this include:

- Quite often members of the Afro-Caribbean ethnic group are working class and therefore material and cultural deprivation can apply, along with the labelling theory.

- The Chinese and other Asian ethnic groups tend to value education highly and therefore a students' family will have a high input into their education. Therefore, these students have more pressure on them to do well and subsequently work harder as to not disappoint their families.

Push and pull factors for immigration.

The pull reason for immigration is that if people see better prospects for themselves and their families in another country that this provides a motivation to move there. It is the same reason why people will often wish to move within a country. The push reason is that if people are living in a violent culture especially in wartime that they will wish to move their families and friends to a safer place. This would have happened in the 1930s with the Jewish population in many countries trying to find safety. Sir Nicholas Winton MBE was a British humanitarian who organized the rescue of 669 children, most of them Jewish, from Czechoslovakia on the trains in 1938 to escape the problems. He died in 2015. Amongst the people he helped was a former Labour MP Baron Alfred Dubs. Some sociologists would suggest that we should learn from this experience to help people at the current time especially those from Syria.

The push factor would also have happened in countries such as Kosovo where many Muslims would have feared for their lives. Eventually NATO in 1999 agreed to take action against the Serbs who were responsible for the massacres.

Current scaremongering campaigns about immigrants

The Guardian, in an article published 29th of March 2016, accused the vote leave campaign, which had the then Justice Secretary, Michael Gove, as its leader, of a scaremongering approach because it drew so much attention to the 14 murders and homicides committed by EU citizens in the UK.[9]

A former Conservative Immigration Minister, Damian Green, suggested that the argument was a mixture of chaos and confusion. The idea that we did not have control over our borders was condemned, since almost 6000 nationals of the European economic area had been stopped from entering the UK since 2010. A former president of the Association of Chief police officers, Sir Hugh Orde, suggested that membership of the European Union was vital to Britain's security, and that around 7000 suspects from the UK have been deported using the European arrest warrant.

Mass migration 2016

In 2016, the migration from Syria, Libya and other war-torn countries as well as the usual economic migrants from a range of countries, meant that large numbers of potential migrants try to enter Europe. The majority of migrants from the war-torn countries had tried to enter and often succeeded in going to countries such as Turkey that were nearer to the conflict. The right-wing media in the UK, as elsewhere, were often very hostile to such migrants. David Cameron, then Prime Minister, had suggested that the majority of aid should go to helping people in the countries from which they came. Additionally, however up to 20,000 migrants from Syria would be allowed into the United Kingdom during the course of the Parliament, which would last up to 2020. Where they would be located would depend partly upon the local authorities involved.

Large numbers of migrants died trying to make the short boat trip from Libya to Europe. Navy vessels including those from the UK were employed to deter the people smugglers. Often the people smugglers received considerable sums of money from potential migrants but the ships themselves were often inadequate and had no safety rafts that could have prevented tragedies had they been provided.

People who are hostile to the migrants suggested that they would be a drain on resources and that infrastructure such as schools and the National Health Service would be inadequate.

There are also exaggerated fears about the security risk.

Ironically, in May 2016, some of the major computer companies in California, United States of America, wanted more skilled migrants, as they could not keep up with the demand for such workers.

Self-examination questions

Q1. Why might families where English is not spoken at home, have a different educational performance to those where English is spoken at home.

Q2. Why might different cultures have different approaches to being ambitious and how might this affect the educational performance?

Q3. Some sociologists have suggested that children who remain in the same area will do better than those who go to a number of different schools in different areas during their school years. Why might this vary according to the ethnic mix?

Q4. What is meant by the term multiculturalism? What would sociologists suggest are the advantages and disadvantages of such a system?

Q5. Sociologists have sometimes suggested that there are both push and pull reasons for immigration. What is meant by this phrase and how far does it explain different patterns of potential immigration to the United Kingdom at this time?

Q6. In 2016, there were many comments about mass migration. What will be the advantages and disadvantages of having radical plans such as helping as far as possible potential immigrants to have better conditions in their home countries?

Q7. Why would terrorist attacks in Brussels and Paris in 2015 affect attitudes towards different ethnic groups? What, if anything, can governments and members of organised religions, including Christianity, Islam and Judaism, do about this?

Q8. Is it relevant to discussions about migration to know that immigrants have proved to be a net economic gain to the UK?

---

8   Max Weber, *The Protestant Ethic and the Spirit of Capitalism*, trans. Talcott Parsons, intro. Anthony Giddens, (London: Routledge, 1992) ISBN 978-0-415-25406-9

9   Anushka Asthana, "Vote Leave releases list of serious crimes by EU citizens in Britain", The Guardian, 29th March 2016, https://gu.com/p/4hqpa

Chapter 5   Gender

Women and class

One of the points made by some feminist writers, as well as by Anthony Giddens in his 1989 book "Sociology"[10] is that women have often not been considered in the writings on class. This is sometimes explained by the idea that women's work has always been considered less important to society as compared to that of men; even though no evidence has generally been produced to suggest this is the case. As the number of single mothers and single women increases, this is even less likely to be true because women are the sole wage earners in the household. The assumption that so-called women's work (looking after the children, cooking, cleaning and general housework) is less important than other duties is a dubious one. The point about housework has been taken up forcefully by feminist writers notably Ann Oakley.

Giddens notes that the issue of gender inequalities overlaps a great deal with class division in men and women. Thus, gender inequalities can substantially be explained by the class system.

Theorizing Patriarchy[11] by Sylvia Walby Defining patriarchy

Walby points out that originally the term 'patriarchy' applied to the idea of older men being in charge of both women and younger men. She is less interested in the generational gap for men, as a definition of the term, and instead concentrates on the more modern usage of the word to mean domination of women by men.

Alternative theories

Walby points out in her 1990 book "Theorizing Patriarchy"[12] there are four theories about patriarchy:

1. The Marxist viewpoint generally identifies women's problems with the capitalist system. Marx assumes that generally the idea of having unpaid housework is helpful to the capitalist since it means that cheap labour is available, whereas if men had to pay women for housework this would not be the case. Walby points out elsewhere that this is the traditional argument and that Marxists assume that women's life is very much tied up with men's.

2. On the other hand, there is the radical feminism school of thought, which would argue that men tend to dominate in society almost irrespective of the system. She points out that radical feminists tend to assume that women have not had a better life, compared to men and that any victories for women are achieved against the wishes of men.

3. The third is the Liberal viewpoint, which tends to suggest a look at individual improvements that have taken place such as the Sexual Offences Act in Kenya.

4. The fourth is the dual system, which tries to integrate the Marxist and the radical feminism viewpoints.

Criticisms of pure Marxist approach

The Marxist viewpoint largely ignores what has happened outside the modern capitalist system. The Kosovan community is still a male-dominated one, even though for a long while Kosovo was part of the communist-dominated world and subsequently it has hardly become modern capitalist. We can also see as Marx himself said that there was patriarchy before modern capitalism anyway.

Marx himself did not study religion very much, and so would not have been able to say much about women's place in Muslim society. Many people have often assumed that women oppressed in Muslim society but this seems to be very different from one country to another. Pakistan has had a female president, the late Benazir Bhutto. Part of the problem with looking at the role of women, purely in class terms is that often many single mothers do not fall into the category of being dependent on the man's income. This may depend upon the level of maintenance, and whether this maintenance is paid. Sometimes a single mother may not have the opportunities as the functionalist would argue to look after herself, but would actually be reliant on the man's income. However, whilst Walby does not say this, it is not clear how many of these women are cohabiting so that they could still be part of male dominated families. In many societies, the number of working women has increased and the tradition of the male breadwinner is no longer so applicable. Sometimes in what might be called 'The sunken middle class' as Douglas notes in one of his books entitled "All Our Future: A Longitudinal Study of Secondary Education" (1970) on sociology of education, is that women might well be earning more than the men anyway. The book is unusual, since it is based on a longitudinal study.

Problems in formulating a general theory

One of the problems in formulating a general theory is that it is unclear that women are necessarily one group. Among the ethnic groups there are quite different work patterns between the Bangladeshi and the Indian, as well as the so-called black women. It could also be argued that this is also true of ethnic groups, which may often have some similar problems but not necessarily a single major cause.

Walby rightly mentions the fact that women on average earn quite a lot less than men do. She does not explain – in spite of her criticism of the functionalist view as being similar to that of the perfect competition model beloved of some economists - why if women receive less pay than men do for equivalent work, firms aiming for bigger profits do not seek to employ women rather than men. The Fawcett Society in 2016 highlighted the slow growth in equal pay for women.

Perhaps part of the answer lies in the research she did in which she cites that often women and men are not doing the same jobs. Walby says that in some cases the social interaction between men, means that women do not hear of jobs that are available through the social grapevines. Though she does not mention it, this may have several other effects, including a tendency for the same grapevines to rule out people from the ethnic groups.

We could go further than this to see how far women and men are doing the same work. In this case, legislation, such as the Sex Discrimination Act 1975 and its subsequent amendments, and the Equality Act 2010, should prevent this. Otherwise, other differences may help to explain the gap. The act covers not only pay, but also promotion and recruitment. She rightly says that even econometric studies have shown that very little of the gap is in terms of what the functionalists have suggested, including economic factors such as difference in qualifications and length of experience. Even at the time Walby was writing her book the differences in qualifications was becoming outdated since at that time girls had overtaken boys in the O levels (the predecessor of the GCSE). It remains to be seen how far changes in women's qualifications affects rates of pay, although if Walby's speculations are valid then there will not be equality if even if – as is happening – women's qualifications are likely to overtake those of men at most levels.

Developments since "Theorizing Patriarchy"

Since the time of Walby's book,[13] it is clear that with far higher staying on rates for A level for both girls and boys, that girls do better at A levels and there seems to be some evidence that girls now do better at first degree level. It is slightly more difficult to be certain of this since the degrees taken tend to be in very different subjects.

The time taken out from work is typically about 5 years for women with children. It seems likely that in view of government measures to encourage women to work (particularly single parents), that this time has probably been reduced. This would mean that if experience is the reason for part of the differences, then this should have been reduced with more provision for nurseries etc.

Since the time of Walby's book[14] that there have been some advances for women, if we look at the 'Blair's babes', that is the number of women who entered parliament particularly in the Labour Party in 1997. The term 'Blair's babes' is extremely patronising, but has been widely used by the tabloids. Less noticed was that in 2004, 6 out of the 12 Liberal Democrat Euro MPs were women.

Walby also noticed the differences in employment rate across the regions; e.g. it is much higher in North West England than for example in South Wales. Since the time of her book, unemployment became lower until the credit crunch 2008 onwards. In 2016, we still have problems of interpreting the data about unemployment however since many women who might be looking for work may not be unemployed according to the government figures since they will not have paid the national insurance contributions which would enable them to have claims for benefits.

Whilst Walby does not say this, we might assume that in a recession that some women might be more likely to work especially if the job prospects for their partners or husbands are bleak.

Walby notes the difference in employment rates between the different regions, which she attributes to the different industries. For example, the North West had a strong textile base that employed women, whereas South Wales had a stronger coal-based employment that was much less likely to employ women. The Welsh valleys are still some of the poorer parts of the UK. It is not however clear how far there were also cultural differences e.g. towards women working in the first place with the South Welsh tradition. It seems possible that the different culture will eventually alter attitudes to work by women, especially as the newer jobs are often white-collar ones rather than manual jobs.

Bucking tradition, women are quietly assuming steadily larger leadership roles across much of Africa. Liberia now has Africa's first elected woman president, Ellen Johnson Sirleaf, a role she has fulfilled since 2006. Mozambique and Sao Tomé and Príncipe have women prime ministers and South Africa and Zimbabwe have female vice presidents. Tanzania has a female foreign minister and women hold at least 30% of the legislative seats in Burundi, South Africa and Mozambique. In Rwanda, women hold 48% of the country's legislative seats. In addition, a woman heads the Supreme Court and half of the country's judges are women, as are half of its college graduates. Similarly, female dropout rates – once high in Rwanda –have plunged after the country's female minister of education began sending social workers to the home of girls who quit school. The workers now try to find schools closer to home for girls who had to walk too far, for instance, or impress on parents that educating girls is as crucial as educating boys.

Sociologists will want to know how wages differ between men and women. Sometimes this could be due to union pressure where the trade unions are powerful enough. Walby makes the point that male trade unionists might be able to exert pressure. It is not however clear why women also could not exert pressure. In other cases, as with clerical work, it could be due to the different locations. Social Trends, shows men are more likely to have access to cars than women are, or even to travel further to work where wages are higher. Hours of work partly account for the differences in gross pay, with men generally being able to put in more hours and overtime at work than women can.

Walby ignores the points made by Professor Hakim that women are not always pursuing the same objectives as men. Professor Hakim states that women have other objectives and that includes preference for more time with children.

Criticism of Harry Braverman

The late Harry Braverman wrote about deskilling of labour. Walby seeks to know why, therefore, such classes as the clerical class have come into this category, without mentioning the gender element since women form a large part of these lower clerical groups. It is, however, unclear whether Braverman's hypothesis is correct, since it could be argued that often new skills have to be learnt. For example, there is no longer scope for big accounts offices in which many women were employed at the lower levels because of the invention of the computer - and its related skills for usage - which has led to this.

Wages could also differ where there are monopolists or oligopsonists that is, either a single or a few buyers of labour respectively. This could apply to the armed forces where governments are the only sources of recruitment or to nursing where governments are amongst the few categories of buyers for this labour market.

This could explain why the armed forces have done comparatively well whereas the teachers have seen their pay fall compared to average earnings.

Violence against women

Walby also writes about violence. She claims, unlike most sociology writers who see violence as an exception and thus the men who commit these crimes are seen as aberration, violence is much more the norm. As she rightly said it is not always obvious how much violence has decreased and whether, for example, an increase in reported crimes are more due to better reporting leading to this apparent decrease. Some people such as Erin Pizzey who formed the first women's refuge at Chiswick in London have suggested that wife beating occurs partly as a cycle of violence.

Ann Oakley makes the points that violence is spread much more evenly across the socio-economic spectrum than most people would probably have thought. She suggests that this is because a lot of violence is not reported. To illustrate this, she quotes Russell as showing that in his survey in the USA, marital rape was consistent across the social spectrum. However, the figures she quotes are American, and it is unclear that these would necessarily apply globally. An article in the Guardian in autumn 2004 (based partly on research by Professor Walby) did however show that violence against women still ran at about two deaths per week in 2004 in the UK. This was some 30 years after the publicity given to violence when Erin Pizzey highlighted the need for women refuges. One commentator suggested that the government seemed more interested in foxhunting and cruelty against foxes, than cruelty against women. It could be argued, though, that abuse against animals may well lead to abuse against people i.e. cruelty is indivisible. Whilst Walby quotes from an alleged Victorian law that the term 'rule of thumb' was the size of the cane that a man could use against a woman it is not clear that such legislation would affect current attitudes. What is perhaps more disturbing was the assumption that women consented to any sex with their husband and it was not until 1991, that is, after Walby's book[15] that there was an offence of marital rape. The argument that few men who committed rape were psychologically disturbed judging by the low rate of referrals to psychiatric help seems to place more reliance on judges' ability at psychology and psychiatry than might have seemed plausible.

Generally, in African countries the concept of 'marital rape' is not accepted by the male members of society. A proposal to criminalize marital rape in Malawi in 2001 sparked a fierce debate in the country. In Kenya, the Sexual Offences Bill was watered down when several male MPs refused to pass the Bill if such concepts of marital rape were left in. Most women therefore rarely report being raped in their marriage bed.

Figures on domestic violence are obviously difficult to determine with accuracy, although they are equally likely to be underestimates rather than overestimates.

Walby correctly makes the point that in most cases, violence against women is not from strangers but from people known to the woman. This has not been helped by the undue prominence given to the few cases of abduction, while the media has generally not acknowledged the extent of domestic violence, except in a few cases such as those involving prominent sportsmen and other celebrities. In the UK, the police, since the release of her book, have taken some steps to ensure women have more of a chance of being heard and treated sympathetically.

The State

Walby shows that even the trade unions have relatively few women in high places. Brenda Dean, Baroness Dean of Thornton-le-Fylde (born 29 April 1943) is an exception to this general rule. She became president of the print union SOGAT in 1983. Dr Mary Bousted was elected president of the TUC in September 2016 replacing another lady who had been the first elected president.

She also suggests that it is difficult for women to be elected in political positions. For instance, in the UK, the House of Commons has not been women friendly; there is a shooting gallery but until recently no crèche.

In Africa, women have for a long time not been expected or encouraged to take up political leadership positions, because traditionally, their sole responsibility was only limited to taking care of the home. She also points out that Marxist feminists have very little to say about the role of women generally.

An example of a female politician

Baroness Williams of Crosby, better known as Shirley Williams, is a former Labour MP who later became a founding member of the SDP, and has sat in the House of Lords as a Liberal Democrat. Her autobiography shows the problems which women face in politics.[16]

Employment

By the year 2008, the UK had more women in employment compared with men. This figure was higher than the EU average at the time, where only 55% of women were employed. Women are far more likely to work part time since in 2008: half of women were employed part time where only one in six men were part time in the UK. Total employment for both men and women as of 2014 was around 30.2 million, this means 77.3% of men and 67.2% of women were in employment. The total of people unemployed in 2014 was just over 2 million.

In 2002, the number of women unemployed was around 700,000 while the number was just under a million for men. For both men and women, the unemployment rate was much higher amongst the young: for 16-17-year-olds, 22% of men and 18.3% of women were unemployed. The number of women unemployed was however lower for all age groups.

20 years ago, the African women's shares in African labour forces ranged from 17%, in Mali, to 49% in Mozambique and Tanzania. They have always been active in agriculture, trade, and other economic pursuits, but a majority of them are in the informal labour force. Though their numbers in the labour force have increased in recent years, they are still lower than those of men are.

Culture

Until recently, sociologists often seemed to suggest that children learnt behaviour that was appropriate for their sex; Walby suggests that this is unhelpful. Many examples on this theory are usually given such as giving girls dolls houses, while boys get toy trains. However, this assumes that people are passive and do not react against this. Presumably, although Walby does not develop this, girls who are very keen to play football will probably eventually get their wishes granted. The assumption that children are always defenceless and never get their own way seems to fly in the way of most observations. Some women presumably would want to be more interested in sport especially if their favourite sports person were to win repeatedly. As Walby points out, the socialisation theory does not indicate where the ideas come from in the first place. It is not obvious in whose interest such socialisation takes place. What would happen if girls were given toy train sets and men were given dolls houses, would their behaviour be different at a later stage? People often write about different styles of dress for men and women, but if we look at the Museum of childhood where it shows children's dress, we sometimes find that what we would regard as female dress has been worn by men.

Some sociologists such as Nancy Chodorow suggest that women get used to nurturing and this is the reason why women become oppressed. Chodorow's remedies are criticised by Walby by saying that men should also take part in parenting. However, this does not necessarily seem reasonable since child rearing is more important than menial work in many factories or the routine jobs within the house such as ironing. The point that Walby makes about the low value given to mothering is perfectly reasonable.

Walby also comments about what she calls the private sphere and public sphere. For instance, she notes that following Florence Nightingale's work in the Crimean war, nursing was a function, which could be carried out by women. She does not however comment about the determination, which Florence Nightingale showed in getting the nursing function recognised.

Walby suggests that women generally could not move out of the women's private sphere, which were generally all female communities and had little or no mixing of genders. She also notes the importance of social workers such as Octavia Hill, 1838 -1912.

Walby suggests there is still a great deal of difference between the subjects, women and men choose to study. It is not clear why this happens or where the different preferences by men and women come from: is it because careers advisers are suggesting only certain jobs for girls or boys? Is it that the parents themselves have decided on the career path they want for their sons or their daughters? Walby also states that some forms of liberalisation have not helped, such as pornography.

She also points out that some jobs have been helped by changes in technology, the moves towards desktop publishing amongst others. The two world wars also made a difference, in that deciding some jobs were unsuitable for women would not have helped in these two periods.

Not all sociologists assume that men and women have identical objectives. Some sociologists, particularly Professor Hakim, have stated that women have other objectives as well.

Gender and exam results

Since 2000, girls have achieved higher results in GCSE's and A-Levels than boys have. However, girls achieve higher results in subjects such as English, while boys generally do better in subjects such as Maths and Physics.

Arguments for this include:
- Girls are said to be more emotional than boys and therefore do better in subjects that reflect emotions, whereas boys do better in subjects that are more hands on.

Stereotyping and exam choices

The current government as with previous ones would like to see more women studying physics and maths so that they can fill up the engineering vacancies which are occurring in spite of an unemployment problem in many regions and total unemployment of around 1.6 million in the UK in mid-2016. Sociologists will be interested in investigating when the stereotypes that women should not study physics or maths occur.

On the other hand, the assumption that women should take part in the performing arts and drama would be common whereas this would be much less likely for men.

The assumption that women should take typing or word processing classes is common since they are much more likely to assume that they will take on secretarial roles rather than become senior managers.

Peer group pressure may also be important since if boys were to go in for dancing they may well be put off by other boys. Billy Elliot, a film, book and musical, emphasises the problems boys would face.

The glass ceiling

The glass ceiling goes against feminist views that males are at an advantage in the educational system as females do actually perform better. However, feminists can argue that this adds to how women are exploited later on in their work life as they have higher qualifications but are still restricted by the glass ceiling and are paid less than men are. The term glass ceiling refers to the idea that women can see the top jobs, but are not usually allowed to take these places. There are still few women at the top in politics in the USA or the UK.

AIDS

AIDS (Acquired Immune Deficiency Syndrome) has become a major indirect killer in many countries. It is indirect since it weakens immune systems. It has been associated with homosexuality, although it is also common with heterosexuals as well.

Prostitution

Prostitution is defined as granting sex for monetary gain. There are debates about whether prostitutes should be prosecuted or whether people should be prosecuted for going with prostitutes. There have been increasing concerns about child prostitution, partly because there are now tours to child prostitutes in other countries such as Thailand. There have also been concerns that child prostitution has become more common in the UK where vulnerable people have allowed children to be used in this way.

Men and women's pay

Robert Half recruiters had an analysis of men's and women's pay, which was shown in an article in the Guardian on March 7, 2016.[17] It was suggested that the typical gap between full-time annual salaries for women and men was £5732 or 24%.

The report suggested that if a career lasted 52 years, then the total shortfall would be £298,064.

This was in in spite of the Sex Discrimination Act 1975 which was meant to ensure that the gaps did not occur. The underlying assumption was that equal work should mean equal pay.

The Fawcett Society, which is a pressure group putting forward the interests of women, thought this was disgraceful.

Similarly, the then TUC secretary Frances O'Grady wanted more action to reduce the U.K.'s gender pay gap.

Sociologists might wish to look at both the employment prospects for women as well, as for wages on an international basis.

The management consultants, PwC, stated that in terms of employment prospects, the UK had climbed to 16th place from 21st, the year before.

Apart from the management reports, feminist sociologists have almost by definition been very interested in the ways that male and female pay has been different, as well as their different working conditions.

Both the First and Second World War, altered the perceptions of what jobs, women could carry out. Typing was originally a male job, and for example until the First World War, there was a separate civil service grade for male typists.

Self-examination questions

Q1. Does the fact that women in the UK are obtaining more jobs than men prove that inequality between sexes has decreased?

Q2. How true is it that there is one general theory explaining why women generally have lower incomes and less power than men do? Would all sociologists agree on this?

Q3. What are the problems of trying to test how income is distributed within the household?

Q4. What is patriarchy?

Q5. What are the diverging theories of patriarchy that have been advanced to-date by various sociologists?

Q6. Why is it difficult to formulate a general theory explaining patriarchy?

Q7. What are the reasons why wages might differ between men and women?

Q8. Figures on domestic violence are difficult to determine with accuracy. Why is this so?

Q9. How far is it true that men and women learn at different speeds for different subjects? Why might it be difficult to test this objectively but why might it be important to do so?

Q10. Why might sociologists be particularly concerned about the extent of child prostitution and its causes?

Q11. Why might gender stereotyping be important for both education and careers choices? How can sociologists assist the government if it is trying to change these perceptions?

Q12. How can sociologists test whether women's and men's objectives are identical? Which well-known sociologists disagree on this and why is this important?

Q13. Why are differences between men and women's pay of interest to sociologists?

Q14. What is a pressure group?

Q15. Why might higher wages for women be helpful to the economy as a whole?

Q16. Why might better-qualified women consider working abroad rather than staying in the United Kingdom?

Q17. What obstacles would there be to women emigrating?

---

10 Anthony Giddens, *Sociology* (London: Macmillan, 1989) ISBN 978-0-333-42739-2
11 Sylvia Walby, *Theorizing Patriarchy* (Oxford: Blackwell, 1990) ISBN 978-0-631-14769-5
12 Ibid.
13 Ibid.
14 Ibid.
15 Sylvia Walby, *Theorizing Patriarchy* (Oxford: Blackwell, 1990) ISBN 978-0-631-14769-5
16 Shirley Williams, *Climbing the Bookshelves: The Autobiography of Shirley Williams* (London: Virago, 2009) ISBN 9781844084760
17 Katie Allen, "Gender pay gap: women earn £300,000 less than men over working life", The Guardian, 7th March 2016, https:// gu.com/p/4hb6x

Chapter 6   Family

A family can be defined as a married couple, civil partners or cohabiting couples, with or without dependent children. It also includes lone parents with dependent children. As secularisation in many countries including the United Kingdom has increased, social attitudes are changing, sociologists often use the term 'families' rather than 'family' to recognise the diversity of family types in today's society.

Data about families in the United Kingdom from the office for national statistics

- In 2014, there were 18.6 million families in the UK. Of these, 12.5 million were married-couple families. This is the most common family type in the UK

- Cohabiting-couple families grew by 29.7% between 2004 and 2014. This is the fastest growing type of family in the UK

- In 2014, there were 2.0 million lone parents with dependent children in the UK. Women accounted for 91% of lone parents with dependent children

- There were 26.7 million households in the UK in 2014. 28% of these contained only one person

- Households containing two or more families were the fastest growing household type in the decade to 2014, increasing by 56% to 313,000 households

Family Diversity

There are five main types of families evident in today's society, however not every family will come under one of these headings. These five are:

Nuclear families

This unit is made up of a married or cohabiting male and female with their biological or adopted children. These are often known as cereal packet families.

Extended families

This unit is made up of over two generations, also with siblings.

There is a link between extended families and the type of work they do. Prior to the agricultural and industrial revolutions in the United Kingdom in the 18th century the household was often the workplace since many rural dwellers had access to small plots of land on which they could grow basic foods. Additionally, people could graze animals on the common lands. A sarcastic comment in the 18th century about the enclosure movement, which meant that commons were often no longer available for ordinary workers, was that "people could be hung for taking sheep from the fields but there were no sanctions against the people who had taken the commons from the people".

Similarly, before the Industrial Revolution many extended families carried out weaving and spinning within the households.

More recently often two or more generations would have worked together in a retail outlet. Living over the shop was very common in many towns and villages.

Extended families are generally made up of a mother, father and their children, also with their parents (the child's grandparents) and the parents' siblings.

Lone parent families

This unit is made up of one parent, either male or female, with their child or children.

Gay or lesbian families

This unit is made up of two adult members of the same sex, with or without children.

Reconstituted families

This unit is made up of two families who come together when the adults get married and the families subsequently become step relations.

Households

A household can be defined as a person living alone or with others in a house or flat. This is different from a family as not all households are families, it is common for friends to live together, especially when house prices or rents are high compared with typical earnings.

The Functionalist View of the Family

As functionalists usually only see the positives in society, they claim that every institution within society works together to benefit the whole of society. They claim that the family acts as a warm bath for its members as they are able to come home and relieve work or school stresses.

Functionalists often ignore family diversity and favour the nuclear family as they claim it performs essential functions. These are:

Primary socialisation

The nuclear family provides role models for children, which can teach them basic behaviour patterns, speech and skills that will be needed later on in life. The family is the first agency of socialisation that a child receives and it is therefore important to get this right.

The nuclear family produces the majority of the policy next generation of the population in society.

Economic Support

As there are two adults in a nuclear family, one or both will be able to support the family financially. This is traditionally the role of the man as he is commonly the breadwinner of the family.

The economic support may be indirect; as many young people, do not know how to handle money once, they have left school. The books "world of work "and "introduction to the world of work by David Spurling may be helpful ""Training young people about this may be part of the family upbringing. Debt problems have been on the increase particularly since the credit crunch 2007 onwards.

Having problems with debt is nothing new. Charles Dickens the famous novelist was aware of debtors' prisons as his father had been in one.

Emotional Support

As there are two adults in a nuclear family, one or both will be able to support the family emotionally. This is traditionally the role of the woman as she is commonly the parent who stays at home to look after the children and household.

The New Right View of the Family

The New Right approach agrees with the functionalist view that the nuclear family is the most beneficial for the family. The approach also reinforces traditional gender roles and suggests that women should take on the caring role within the family, while the men should be the breadwinners to provide financial support.

The New Right recognises family diversity but still claims that the nuclear family works best, while claiming that the other types are damaging for society. This is because families who lack role models for children, for example lone parent families where a man is not present can cause a child to grow up in delinquency and disrespect. This can be argued that it is because traditionally the man of the house would administer discipline and therefore the child never learns right from wrong. However, it can also be argued that a parent who does not care can cause emotional distress for the child. Emotional neglect is more difficult to define but is still important.

The Marxist View of the Family

Marxists criticise the nuclear family as they claim it maintains capitalism. They have developed some arguments for this. Firstly, they claim that the nuclear family supplies future generations of workers as they all follow the norms and values of people who capitalists exploit. Similarly, they also claim that the nuclear family socialises working class children to obediently accept their low position in an unfair society. This not only gives them an idea of where they should belong but reduces the motivation for social mobility. One other argument Marxists use is that members of the upper class can buy their children an education that the working class cannot afford and therefore adds to social class reproduction. Non-Marxists might comment that in many cases the children in China, and even more in North Korea, would receive an education that was both expensive and kept them away from ordinary members of those societies.

The Feminist View of the Family

Feminists criticise the nuclear family as they claim it is based on patriarchy. It gives men a chance to exploit women through power and dominance. When this behaviour occurs within a family, it is much harder to escape from such violence. Feminists also criticise the functionalist view of the warm bath theory as it gives men an opportunity to take their frustrations from work out on women.

They will be aware of the sexual abuse, which has taken place in many societies including the United Kingdom.

Gender Roles

Different sociologists have argued as to whether gender roles in families have significantly changed since the 1960s.

Sociologists who support the claim that gender roles have changed over time

Young and Willmott (1973) argue that the symmetrical family is the most common in Britain today. This is not just roles within the household but also power roles including decision making with money.

Gatrell (2008) found that fathers now have more of an input in their children's lives than in the past.

Sociologists who claim that gender roles have not changed over time

Crompton and Lyonette (2008) argue that men's input into the household care has not increased as much as women's career paths. They also offer the suggestion that it is more of a case that women spend less time completing housework, rather than men doing more of it. They also argue that although men may help more around the house, there are still certain chores that are seen as a woman's job, such as washing and ironing.

Division of Labour

Social scientists sometimes use the phrase division of labour to investigate how the jobs in the household are split up. They would suggest that women often do the administrative tasks within the family such as making appointments to see medical staff, dentists and educational staff rather than the men doing this.

Changing nature of the family

A Guardian article on March 19th 2016 suggested that for many younger people, who it labelled generation K, family was less important than technology.[18] The article by Noreena Hertz suggested that the new generation are much more likely to be involved in both multi-screening and multi-tasking. The evidence that they are troubled was bought out in a World Health Organisation report in March 2016, which on a survey of 42 nationalities suggested that only teenagers from Macedonia and Poland are less happy with life than UK people.

Many of them worry about getting a job and getting into debt. They are also concerned about terrorism, even though most of them will not have had any first-hand experience, but the mass media, which they are constantly watching, has had its effect. In spite of the technology, 80% of people interviewed by the Guardian reporter suggested that they prefer being with their friends in person rather than being on line.

Changing parent-child relationships

The raising of the school leaving age to 18 in the UK from 2015 means children will be more financially dependent upon their family for a longer period than their predecessors. The imposition of University tuition fees and the far greater proportion of children going to universities or other forms of higher education than in previous generations will also reinforce this. However, in some family businesses, children may help, officially or unofficially, even before they have left school.

Some people have referred to the boomerang generation i.e. students may go away to University but will then come back to the family home after this.

The increase in average house prices and rents compared with typical earnings means that younger people will find it much more difficult generally to move away from home than in the past.

More details about house prices and earnings can be found from the Nationwide Building Society website.

Grandparents support

Grandparents may support families in a of different ways. They may be able to provide babysitting services for parents who might otherwise not be able to get the jobs that they wish. They may also be involved in informal teaching which may be helpful to young people. As the number of people who have been evicted from their homes because they have defaulted on mortgages or loans has often increased, they may be able to provide shelter to their children and their grandchildren when otherwise they could be homeless.

They may also be able to provide a listening service that children trust when they have emotional problems.

How much support grandparents may give may also depend on the ethnic group. Extended families living in the same area or sometimes the same house will differ considerably in their patterns of behaviour depending partly upon race. The Indian subcontinent community will often give more support than the indigenous population.

Alternative family structure

In Israel, particularly after the establishment of the state after 1948 many families belonged to Kibbutzim where the children were bought up in a community rather than by individual parents. Part of the logic of this was that men and women were free to work on equal terms. However, fewer people now work in such settings.

There are also other communities such as the L' Arche community which exists in several places including Canterbury.

It relies heavily on volunteers to look after people with some disabilities who otherwise find it difficult to obtain jobs and live a normal life. More details can be found on their website.

Some people have decided that they do not like what they regard as the rat race, and may live in a community such as the ones Rudolf

Steiner (1861 – 1925) formed or the Iona community, which was founded by the Rev George MacLeod in 1938 and is associated with the Church of Scotland. He took people from a poor Dockland parish in Govan, Glasgow, as well as young trainee clergy who worked together to build the monastic quarters of a medieval abbey, working together as they did so. Iona is a small island off the west coast of Scotland.

Bringing up children

Sociologists views on bringing up children

Sociologists will have a number of ideas about how children should be brought up. They will be concerned about the number of dysfunctional families that exist in the United Kingdom. They will be aware of important ideas, which have often been accepted by many educationalists.

Jean Piaget

Jean Piaget (1896-1980) was a well-known Swiss psychologist who specialised in theories about child development, but it was not until the 1960s that his ideas became widely publicised.

He had stated in 1934, that only education would save our societies from possible collapse.

Sociologists will be aware that the birth of the child, whether it is the first child or subsequent one will drastically change the nature of the family. However, they will also be interested to ensure that unnecessary stillbirths do not take place. Sociologists will be aware that having as far as possible a smoke-free atmosphere during pregnancy will reduce the risk of miscarriages and stillbirths.

They will also be aware that women should desist from harmful drugs since there are many studies showing the effects of these on the number of stillbirths.

Women should be aware of the risks, such as the Zika virus which has mainly centred on Brazil, but which has received wide publicity in many other places, about the deficiencies that can occur if women are affected by the disease.

Sociologists will also be aware that jealousies can occur with abusive partners and, whilst headlines about murders hit the headlines, it is more difficult to know how many miscarriages have taken place because of violent abuse.

Many women would like to be able to breastfeed but is a rather odd example of primness in the United Kingdom that some other people find it embarrassing if women do this in public.

Women can obtain good advice from the National Childbirth Trust (NCT), which offers a range of suitable publications as well as advice on its website.

Increasingly men also want to take part in the upbringing of small children and there is currently legislation about paternity leave, details of which can be found on government websites.

Grandparents can often help if they are willing with the informal and sometimes formal education of children. This may help to relieve pressure on the parents who may otherwise be torn between having a career and parental responsibilities. Children are naturally curious and can often be helped to develop manual dexterity with suitable toys such as Lego and Duplo.

Changing family patterns

In the United Kingdom and in the USA, there are far more divorces than in the past. The number of divorces in England and Wales rose from 25,394 in 1961 to 243,818 in 2001 but fell to 117,558 in 2011.

Divorces generally, are now decreasing in the United Kingdom, across most age groups although not in the so-called grey groups.

Can the government help to reduce the divorce rate?

Sociologists have suggested in the United Kingdom that more couples should have to have mediation to avoid the stress that divorce causes. Other people however have suggested that the state should not be involved in personal decisions. The counterargument to this is that often the state pays out more in Social Security because of divorce. It also adds to the housing shortage. This is because when divorce takes place more accommodation is generally required than when the couple live together.

Reasons for the long term increase in divorce rates

The changes in the divorce rate may be partly because churches such as the Roman Catholic Church, which is generally opposed to divorce, have become less important. The divorce reform act 1969 in the UK meant that if there was an irretrievable breakdown of marriage this would-be grounds for divorce.

In 1984, people could petition for divorce after one year of marriage rather than three years.

However, it could be argued that the number of divorces led to the acts being passed rather than the acts led to the number of divorces increasing.

It may also be because women have a greater chance of obtaining jobs and therefore are less likely to be willing to remain in the empty shell marriage. This term applies to marriages where there is little relationship either emotional or sexual between the couple, but they remain married, perhaps because of the expense of divorce.

Marriage rates in the United Kingdom

Fewer people are getting married; this may be the result of the influence of the churches falling in British society. It may also be because women no longer have to find a husband in order to have a reasonable income.

Older age of marriage

Both women and men are getting married at an older age. Data about this can be found in government publications. This may be partly because women often want to have a career before they get married. It may also be because increasing house prices in many areas means that it is difficult for couples to be able to afford suitable accommodation even if they wish to get married.

Smaller number of children in the family

Smaller numbers of children are being born to the typical family in the United Kingdom. This may be partly because of the older age of marriage and that, having postponed having a child, not all women will be able to have children at a later stage even if they wish to. IVF treatments for women may possibly alter this in the future. The fertility rates vary between different ethnic groups with generally the Indian subcontinent population having a greater number.

More men and women are resorting to cohabitation and government publications shows that this is very common in the United Kingdom.

Bringing up children

Sociologists should be able to give advice to governments and parents and/or guardians on this important topic.

Children's life chances will be improved if there are sufficient midwives who can give suitable advice to pregnant mothers before the children are born. This would include ideas such as not smoking or taking drugs or having excessive amounts of alcohol during pregnancy. Sociologists would be aware of the statistical data, which shows the risks if this advice is not followed.

Children need to get rewards for good behaviour in order to stimulate them. Most sociologists would suggest that a positive approach to children helps them. One of the problems in modern society is that excessive fear about strangers can mean that children are not allowed sufficient freedom, which would enable them to become more mature. They need to be able to explore parks and open spaces especially when they are known to be safe areas.

They need to be able to learn to assess risks.

They need to be kept away from cleaners such as detergents also deodorants, medicines and sharp objects. It may be important to lock cupboards. As they get older, parents and guardians have to move dangerous items out of the way. It is also important that children be kept away from heavy things, which can fall on them. They need to be kept away from electrical equipment.

They also need to be kept away from any animals that could be dangerous. Unfortunately, there have been many incidents where dangerous pets have bitten, or very occasionally killed, children. Whilst there has been legislation about dangerous dogs, it is often used once an incident has occurred rather than to prevent dangerous dogs being allowed in the first place.

Despite media reports suggesting stranger danger is the main problem, more children are killed and injured in road accidents in the UK than from such causes.

At a very early stage in life children need to be kept clean and potty trained parents and guardians need to agree on what rules should be played otherwise there is a temptation for the children to manipulate parents by playing off mum and dad. This is particularly likely to happen after a separation or divorce.

By the age of three, most children have a vocabulary of about 300 words. Research shows that if children have been stimulated, whether within the family or within good childcare facilities, they are much more likely to have achieved this than if they are simply plonked in front of the television or otherwise encouraged to remain passive. It is important to keep children especially very young ones from being either too hot or too cold. Preventing them from being too cold is comparatively easy although you do not want children to be indoors all the time. Having several layers of clothes is helpful rather than heavy clothes, and some firms are very good at selling cheap but effective waterproof clothes, which let your skin breathe rather than making you very sweaty.

Children need fresh air but need to avoid being out in the sun for too long a period, since it is possible to get skin cancer (particularly melanoma) if they do not have suitable protection in the way of clothing and possibly sun cream as well. They may need to have hats as well, which many young children do not like.

Children need to wear suitable clothes. At many schools, there may be little option since they may have to wear some form of school uniform. Children should not be encouraged to compete on the most expensive pair of trainers, clothes, since this will often lead to an inferiority complex.

Food

It is important that children are fed at regular intervals and generally it is better to aim at three good meals a day rather than having too many snacks and in particular too many drinks which have a lot of sugar and also too many unhealthy foods such as crisps and other fatty ones. Most foods nowadays have details about how much fat, sugars, etc. are within them, and it is important therefore that parents look at this. However takeaway foods often contain considerable amounts of fat and sugar.

In particular, many children now have developed allergies, which can be harmful, and therefore if it is known that children are allergic to some foods such as nuts et cetera it is important that schools or other people involved with the child's upbringing are advised about this.

Children may also be allergic to some types of soaps, or detergents.

Many children who take school meals with them have some fruit and vegetables, but also too much chocolate.

Schools should be able to provide cold water, which is much better for most people than fizzy drinks, although too often the outside taps have been broken and not repaired.

Children need suitable food and drink although when they are babies they only need milk. A balanced healthy diet is important for children as for people of all ages.

Ideally, it should contain five portions of fruit and vegetables without too much sugar or fat. In spite of all the pressures from supermarkets and other advertisements on television, either directly or indirectly it is important that they do not eat too much junk food since many children are obese before they even reach school age.

Teeth

Sugary foods, as well as acid foods are not very good for children's teeth. Fruit and fruit juice are healthy, but they also have the capacity to hurt children's teeth, so it is helpful if they can be eaten or drunk at lunchtimes or at other mealtimes, rather than part of continuous snacking.

It is important that children learn to clean their teeth at an early age.

Exercise

It is helpful if children are outside some of the time and encouraging them to walk or run or cycle may be helpful.

Even going up and down swings encourages them to let off steam but also gives them some exercise.

Encouraging children to swim may also be helpful.

Having a float might be helpful and, when a bit older, teaching children to dive from the edge of the swimming pool might be good. Having a helter-skelter, where they go straight into the water may be fun, and encourages them to go back into swimming.

Teenagers may be encouraged to take up skateboarding, especially if there is a separate area for them.

Some teenagers may also like to go ice-skating, if there is a suitable rink near them.

Children can be taught to talk by copying their parents. They can listen to people singing or having other suitable music, which can help to smooth children's tempers. Listening to aggressive rap on the other hand, will not improve their behaviour.

Children's early learning

It is important that they are taught basic words and this is frequently done by pointing things out to them. It is important that children are listened to and that their parents do not spend all their time on the mobile phone, the Internet or other gadgets including television.

This does not mean that children should be able to dominate the parents.

Children's leisure activities

In general, it is better for children to be given toys or books, which stimulate the imagination, rather than having the television on all the time. Lego and Duplo are very good for stimulating children since they can build a great variety of different items and it helps them with manual dexterity and imagination.

Some television programmes such as Blue Peter are however educational and children might be encouraged to watch them. Children need to be kept away from using the Internet too much although the Internet is a useful source of information it can also obviously be used to abuse children. Children need to be given treats occasionally and in particular to be encouraged rather than discouraged. Children are often patronised, and it is therefore important that children be allowed to grow up. They need freedom within reasonable limits. They can be taught to walk better by giving them toys at an early age that help them to reach out, rather than parents immediately rushing to help them. It's important to walk around with children so they get to recognise the area in which they live and even at an early age it is helpful if they know their name and address so that if they do get lost they can be quickly brought back to their home.

Safety

Children need to recognise things that are dangerous and those that are safe. In particular, they need to be kept away from cleaners such as detergents as well as deodorants, medicines and sharp objects. It is important that these items are kept in locked cupboards, or at least in cupboards which children cannot easily reach. When they reach toddler stage, they need to have dangerous items moved out of their way since they are by nature inquisitive. In particular, it is important that they are kept away from electrical equipment and suitable safety plugs can be installed. Children can easily be suffocated and therefore it is important to be careful of pillows.

Sociologists will be aware of child cot deaths and data about this can be found on government websites. Children should be kept equally away from plastic bags as these can cause suffocation. At the toddler stage, it is helpful if there can be safety gates near any stairs. Passive smoking is still a considerable risk to small and other children and therefore adults, including parents, should not smoke near small children. There is increasing amount of legislation about smoking in cars. Young children also need to be kept away from very bright lights.

One of the major risks to children is road deaths and accidents and it is important that they soon learn to keep to the pavements and not to cross roads without adequate supervision.

One way of trying to make sure that they do this is that at a toddler age they can be kept on reins as they are in a dangerous area.

It is advisable to teach them the Highway Code as soon as possible. They should learn how to cross roads safely when walking. Road accidents are still a major cause of death in most countries for young people, including the United Kingdom.

At an early stage, it is helpful to get them to be clean and to potty train them as soon as they can reasonably be ready.

Exercise is important for children as well as adults and swimming is often a method of both taking exercise, as well as relaxing. At seaside resorts, it is helpful if children can be kept away from deep water. Many beaches now have beach patrols and it is therefore advisable to ensure that swimming takes place within these limits.

It is important that parents agree on what they want their children to do so that the children do not manipulate parents by playing off mum versus dad or vice versa. Sociologists will be well aware of Freudian psychology and even if not accepting all the premises will know that boys often will get around their mums and girls will often manipulate their dads.

Increase in the number of stay at home dads

A survey in 2010 stated that 1.4 million men were primary carers for their children, and this was 10 times the number in 2000.

Longitudinal studies of parenting in society

The National Child Development Survey, NCDS, is a longitudinal study which started in 1958 and looks at a representative sample of children born in that year. As with other longitudinal studies, it has the advantage of looking in depth at people's behaviour.

It tried to trace all members of this birth generational cohort periodically between 1965 and 2014, to get information concerning their physical, educational and social development. It has looked at a wide variety of factors and topics including medical care as well as family relationships and originally stillbirths.

In 1985, the NCDS was moved to the Social Statistics Research Unit (SSRU), which is now known as the Centre for Longitudinal Studies.[19][20]

Resilience

Sociologists as well as other academics and social workers have often used the word resilience when looking at both families and individuals. The advantage of this is that it offers a more positive approach in seeing how good outcomes can arise even if problems would normally be expected.

Sociologists will need to develop theories, which need to be tested by looking at empirical investigations. The term resilience denotes how people have the capacity to deal with difficult circumstances and how can adapt to changes in their lives. Parental and foster parental attitudes may be important. Similarly, schools can help by praising what is right rather than concentrating on what is wrong.

An example of this would be that if social services are placing a foster child with a new family that they might say, "You have now an opportunity to have more brothers and sisters." This would be in contrast to the over timid approach which assumes that the child will not get on with any siblings.

Self-examination questions

Q1. What is meant by the nuclear family? Why might the children and others in the nuclear family have a different pattern of behaviour to the extended family?

Q2. What is meant by the reconstituted family? Why might there be more tensions in this type of family than in some others?

Q3. What views do the functionalists have about the family? What evidence do they have to support these views?

Q4. What views does "The New Right" hold about the family? How if at all can government actions influence the patterns of families?

Q5. Why might sociologists be interested in the happiness or unhappiness of younger generations in the United Kingdom? What advice can they therefore give the government to see if happiness can be improved?

Q6. What is meant by the boomerang generation? What are its causes and is it desirable?

Q7. Why have sociologists been interested in the distribution of household jobs within the family? Why might it be difficult to get accurate data about this? Why might it vary between different social classes and different regions?

Q8. Why might changing higher prices of houses and other accommodation affect the family structure?

Q9. Why might sociologists be interested in how much domestic violence there is in society? Why might it be difficult to get accurate data about the extent of this?

Q10. What would be the advantages and disadvantages of bringing up children in a community rather than in individual families?

Q11. Why would sociologists be interested in the divorce rate in the UK and other countries? Some sociologists and others have suggested that more mediation should be used rather than any other methods to try to reduce the rate. What would be the advantages and disadvantages of this?

Q12. Why would changes in employment patterns have an impact upon the family?

Q13. Why might grandparents be able to help some families and in what ways? Why might this differ between different ethnic groups?

Q14. Some societies value older people, since they have experience that can be used to help the young. Would it be better in the UK rather than assuming that older people have nothing to give that they are regarded as an asset rather than a drain on society?

Q15. What advice can sociologists give on how children can be bought up to be safe but happy? Why might use of primary and secondary data be helpful when giving such advice?

Q16. Sometimes the courts have ordered parents to attend good parenting classes. These classes can give information about how to buy goods and services sensibly. Is this an example of excessive meddling by the state or a good example of a proactive rather than a reactive approach?

Q17. Why might longitudinal studies be helpful when investigating children's upbringing?

Q18. What is meant by the term stillbirths and what advice can sociologists give local and central government about methods to reduce this?

Q19. What is meant by the term resilience and why might sociologists be interested in this?

Q20. What sources of stress are likely to occur in typical families and how can the effects of these be reduced?

---

18 Noreena Hertz, "Think millennials have it tough? For 'Generation K', life is even harsher", The Guardian, 19th March 2016, https://gu.com/p/4hk8q

19 Centre for Longitudinal Studies, "Welcome to the 1958 National Child Development Study", UCL Institute of Education, https://www.cls.ioe.ac.uk/page.aspx?sitesectionid=724

20 Wikipedia contributors, "National Child Development Study," Wikipedia, https://en.wikipedia.org/wiki/National_Child_Development_Study

Chapter 7 — Social class and mobility

Sociologists sometimes refer to social class, and sometimes to social stratification.

Some societies, such as Greece at the time of its greatest influence from around 400 BC, and Rome from around 50 BC until around 400 CE, were founded mainly upon slavery. Slaves were sold in the same way as any other commodity, and we can find descriptions of their physical and mental characteristics. It might be thought that slavery was a thing of the past, but in recent years in the United Kingdom, there has been an anti-slavery Act mainly because people have been lured to the United Kingdom on the assumption of good jobs and accommodation and then being kept in virtual slavery.

The Modern Slavery Act 2015 consolidated previous legislation about trafficking and slavery. It was sponsored by Theresa May the then Conservative Home Secretary.

Feudal society existed throughout most of Europe at the time of William the conqueror who became King of England in 1066 after the battle of Hastings. In this system, there was a hierarchy with king at the top and everybody else having allegiance to a person above them. The feudal system collapsed in England, mainly because of the Black Death. This was a bubonic plague, which reached England in 1348 but died down in 1349, which killed perhaps half the population so that there were not enough people to maintain the system. In some countries, particularly in India, there has been a caste system, which is much more rigid than the ordinary class system, since people cannot change their caste. In 2016, there have been protests by people from the lowest caste in Delhi, the biggest city in India, and this has resulted in problems for the water supply, since the canal system has been sabotaged.

Mahatma Gandhi, who was the first president of India immediately after Indian independence in 1947, wished to improve the lot of the lowest caste the Davits, but did not completely succeed.

Whereas Karl Marx assumed that there were two main classes, i.e. the rich and the proletariat, most modern sociologists would suggest that there are three classes, i.e. the richest, the middle class who have become increasingly numerous and important, and also the working class.

Sociologists have been interested in class, partly because so many differences in society depend upon the social class. If sociologists look at government publications they can see the differences in life expectancy between the different classes. In particular, sociologists can look at the differences in infant mortality, not just in the United Kingdom, but in many others. We can also look at the differences in house ownership as well as the differences in voting behaviour.

Whereas the majority of the middle class own their own homes, the working class are more often found in council housing, although more recently this role has been taken over by housing associations.

However, voting behaviour over time has changed so that no longer do working class people necessarily vote for the Labour Party and the middle class for the Conservative Party. The increasing influence of the Scottish National Party after the general election in 2015 meant that the Labour Party only had one Scottish seat in the Westminster Parliament. In the local elections, there are even greater disparities between the different parties. At the European Parliament elections in 2014, there were even more differences with UKIP having obtained the largest share of the vote. We can still find people voting in different ways at different levels so that people may vote one way in local elections, another way in general elections, and a different way in the European elections.

How can we classify people into classes?

One of the most common ways that sociologists classify people is by occupations.

Occupations are used, partly because they give an indication of both salaries or wages and prestige. There is a strong link as well between education and types of job. However, there are some reservations about job titles and occupations, the term engineer may be used to denote people who have no particular skills or may also indicate people who belong to the various organisations such as electrical engineer's mechanical engineers and so on. Similarly, even the word farmer may mean the very rich, such as the Duke of Westminster, or a hill farmer with a small patch of poor land where a subsistence-style living from a few sheep gives a low level of income.

If we look at the hierarchy of wages, we can see that some jobs such as cleaners and personal carers are poorly paid, whilst other jobs, such as those working as accountants for the big six accounting firms, receive very large sums of money. There is now a national minimum wage and the Conservative government has announced that it intends to have a national living wage. This came into effect on April 1, 2016.

The richest members of society, however, frequently do not have to do any jobs so that we cannot define them on this basis.

For a considerable period, the registrar general classified people into five main classes:

I. At the top social class, class I, were professionals and executives. This included for example, doctors and accountants.
II. In class II were semi-professional managers including teachers and nurses.
III. In class III (N) were skilled non-manual workers such as clerks. In class III (M) were skilled manual workers including carpenters.
IV. In class IV were semiskilled manual workers
V. In class V were unskilled manual workers.

The Office for National Statistics (ONS), which is independent of the government, now classifies people into a different category of classes.
1. Higher managerial, administrative and professional occupations
   1.1 Large employers and higher managerial and administrative occupations
   1.2 Higher professional occupations

2. Lower managerial, administrative and professional occupations

3. Intermediate occupations

4. Small employers and own account workers

5. Lower supervisory and technical occupations

6. Semi-routine occupations

7. Routine occupations

8. Never worked and long-term unemployed

The BBC now suggests from 2013:[21]
- Elite
  The most privileged group in the UK, distinct from the other six classes through its wealth. This group has the highest levels of all three capitals.

- Established middle class
  The second wealthiest, scoring highly on all three capitals. The largest and most gregarious group, scoring second highest for cultural capital.

- Technical middle class

A small, distinctive new class group which is prosperous but scores low for social and cultural capital. It is distinguished by its social isolation and cultural apathy.

- New affluent workers
A young class group which is socially and culturally active, with middling levels of economic capital.

- Traditional working class
Scores low on all forms of capital, but is not completely deprived. Its members have reasonably high house values, explained by this group having the oldest average age at 66.

- Emergent service workers
A new, young, urban group which is relatively poor but has high social and cultural capital.

- Precariat, or precarious proletariat
The poorest, most deprived class, scoring low for social and cultural capital.

Many sociologists would suggest that class differences are not as great as they used to be. One phrase for this is embourgeoisement, which means that the working class have often adopted a middle-class attitude. However, other sociologists such as Goldthorpe would not accept that this has happened.

The rich not only earn considerably more than the other classes, but, often also have considerable wealth.

In January 2016, Oxfam, the well-known charity, stated that the richest 62 people in the world owned as much wealth as the poorest half of the world's population. This is often due to the rich inheriting wealth rather than because of their earnings in their lifetime. More details about the richest people can be found in Forbes and on their website. Bill Gates, the well-known developer of computer software was still the richest person in 2015. In 2016 however he announced that the Bill Gates foundation would give away most of his money.

Sociologists also use the phrase "white-collar workers" to mean those people who work in offices or retail establishments etc. The nature of white-collar jobs has changed considerably since increasingly computers have changed both the numbers of people employed on particular processes and the types of jobs that are being done.

Routine bookkeeping, which provided many jobs in many organisations, is now usually computerised so that the main task is keying in information.

Whereas shop assistants' jobs were often low-paid, they were regarded as secure jobs until the 1960s, but increasingly online shopping means that the number of people at the tills has declined rapidly and this trend is likely to continue.

Blue-collar jobs have also changed; the number of people being employed in coal mining has dwindled considerably. The number of people working on the land has also fallen, so that the routine work, which provided holiday jobs such as those on the hop picking fields in Kent, requires far fewer people. In many cases, fruit picking is carried out by migrant workers who are more prepared to do unpleasant jobs.

The fishing industry employs far fewer people, although the future number had depended upon the European Union's fishing policy (CFP). It is unclear following Brexit what the UK will do.

Many sociologists and other social scientists are concerned that, because of computers, automation and robots, people without qualifications or skills will be permanently unemployed.

Partly for this reason both the current Conservative government, the previous coalition government and previous Labour party administrations have wished to see more people take up apprenticeships, so that people can both gain work experience as well, as formal qualifications.

In particular, in spite of high rates of unemployment in the UK and elsewhere many engineering jobs are still vacant and therefore the government would like to see people being trained to take up these vacant positions.

Social mobility

Karl Marx assumed that the main distinction between the classes was that of property ownership. Those who had property would usually inherit the money, and therefore the landed classes would continue to prosper, whilst the other class, the proletariat would become generally poorer as the economy had greater fluctuations.

Critics of Karl Marx would suggest however that he ignored the increasing number of people who belonged to the bourgeois. The joint stock company meant that often companies became bigger and people with talents could become highly paid managers, without necessarily having had any wealth to start with.

Some sociologists have used the term meritocracy, particularly the late Lord Young. They would suggest that people such as the former Conservative Prime Minister Sir Edward Heath was an example of someone from a relatively poor background, succeeding to get one of the highest positions in the United Kingdom.

Critics of this viewpoint would suggest that, before the referendum in 2016, the then Prime Minister David Cameron, and his Chancellor of the Exchequer, George Osborne, were educated at Eton. Similarly, the Levenson report highlighted the number of people at the top, in politics, the media or the law, who came from privileged backgrounds.

One of the reasons why the school leaving age is now 18 (with exceptions for people who undertake apprenticeships or go to technical colleges or have home tutoring) is that it is hoped by doing this, that more people will be able to proceed to the highest jobs.

If we wish to find suitable jobs for people who are currently "anti-school", one problem is that we do not always know what future jobs there will be.

This means that syllabi need to be updated to take account of changes and also we may need to have more joint studying since few people work in isolation.

We might need open book examinations since otherwise many exams are merely a test of memory and we may need to consider whether we actually need hand written exams.

There is a possibility of problems if computers are allowed, but there are already problems with plagiarism.

In the deviant subculture, sociologists such as Paul Willis suggest that working-class boys improved their status through a deviant behaviour that they would not have gained if they had done well at school.

Sociologists can also see anecdotal evidence about this. For example, if television crew are apparent, where there have been examples of gang violence, some of the group will be willing to play up to this image. The same will apply to people being interviewed on the radio.

Some Marxists however, will suggest that labelling theory results in working class boys in particular being labelled as criminals because the people who deal with them whether magistrates or judges, probation officers, police officers or people from the schools whether teaching staff or administrative staff will label students as failures, whereas teenage boys who behave in the same way will not be labelled in the same way.

Apart from the concept of class, sociologists can see that the same groups in schools and people concerned with maintaining the law will often react in different ways to people from different cultures.

Research suggests that class, rather than ethnic background, is more likely to correlate with school performance.[22]

Self-examination Questions on Class

Q1. Why was slavery so prevalent in much of Roman society?

Q2. Why has the UK government introduced an antislavery Bill?

Q3. Why did feudal society end after the Black Death in England in the 14th century?

Q4. Why have sociologists been interested in social mobility?

Q5. What is meant by the caste system? What happens to social mobility in such a system? Why might this prevent India performing as well, as it could do?

Q6. Outline some of the different views sociologists have about class. Why is it difficult to determine which of these are correct?

Q7. Why is infant mortality different between different social classes? What could be done, to reduce the mortality in the lowest classes, and what obstacles are there to such reductions?

Q8. Sociologists have sometimes suggested that occupation is the easiest way to assess to which social classes people belong. Why might this not be quite as easy as might be first thought?

Q9. Why have women often found it difficult to get to the top in commerce, politics, and other spheres?

Q10. What is the link between educational performance in the different ethnic groups and their aspirations?

Q11. Why are sociologists interested in the ways that some groups, such as the Chinese, want their children to achieve far more than the indigenous UK population?

---

21 BBC News, "Huge survey reveals seven social classes in UK", 3rd April 2013, http://www.bbc.com/news/uk-22007058
22 Jessica Shepherd, "Social class affects white pupils' exam results more than those of ethnic minorities – study", The Guardian, 3rd September 2010, https://gu.com/p/2jdk8

Chapter 8   Changing patterns of work

If sociologists look at patterns of work before the industrial revolution, they will find that in rural areas many families were mainly self-sufficient since they could graze animals on the commons or sometimes agree to work together for example at harvest time but wages would have been comparatively unimportant. In other countries, slavery would be common, and in the England, after the Norman Conquest in 1066, the people at the bottom of the ladder would have been slaves in all but name.

In the 20th century and early 21st century, white-collar jobs have become much more important, and women have increasingly taken up the white-collar jobs. In recent years, the concept of flexible skills has become more important, the assumption is that people will have to change occupation or industries during their working life. Flexible skills will mean that the educational system in turn needs to adapt so that there will be continuous professional development. Whilst this may be required if people change occupations they may require different skills to those in their current organisations. The concept of Just-in-time is important. This puts considerable strains on the supply chain which means the distribution industry and the distribution process.

Women are increasingly important in the workforce, and are much more likely to be involved in certain professions. This means the distinction between work and non-work becomes more blurred since within the family women have often been the teachers or secretaries and they maintain these roles as well in their work. Increasingly women have married at a later age and have had fewer children as well as having children at a later age.

The disabled have often faced restrictions on the jobs they can do. The advent of ICT and working from home, may mean that they have a wider choice of jobs available.

For both men and women life expectancy has increased significantly. Men have often taken early retirement resulting in skill shortages, especially in engineering. The assumption that people may be able to work 30 years from the age of 20+ to their late 50s and then have an adequate pension is implausible. The government has subsidised pension contributions, and, from 2015, people may choose to spend this pension pot on whatever they wish rather than having to purchase an annuity. However, part of the problem is that people underestimate their life expectancy.

Changing nature of women's employment

In the 19th century partly because of the factory acts (including the 1842 act) and legislation about work in the coalmines (1844), women were not allowed to do some jobs. Prior to the industrial revolution it had been common for families to work as groups whether in the mines or in agriculture or in the home textile industry. Apart from legislation, there were also conventions that prevented women working as shop assistants.[23] Women were not normally considered suitable to be employed as shop assistants, although 19th century census data showed that sometimes women would have had an informal role helping other members of the family. They were considered unsuitable, partly because of lack of physical strength. The 19th century convention at the time was that shop assistants would always have to stand. Later research showed the extent of physical pain and injuries caused to women as shop assistants by this need to stand.[24] The two world wars altered the ideas of what women could do. Typing had been predominantly a male occupation until 1914. This was partly because the original typewriters required some physical strength but also because of the convention that secretaries should be male. The civil service had a special grade for male typists. Until the First World War, many women had been in service, which was the euphemism for being a servant. In contrast to the romantic approach to domestic service in the TV series 'Downton Abbey' many employers were very abusive. In the Second World War, many women were recruited as land girls so that food production could continue since many men were recruited into the army. Many women also worked in munition and gunpowder factories. In the First World War, the Military Service Act 1916 was passed which was the first time ever that conscription had been applied in England, Wales and Scotland. It did not apply in Ireland because of political sensitivity. Conscription applied to males between the age of 18 and 45 so that the male jobs needed women to replace them although after the First World War there were pressures from both the trade unions and employers that they did not wish women to continue in some of these jobs. Women became conductresses on the buses and worked in some railway jobs, since public transport was vital to get both members of the armed forces and munition to the places required. The large number of deaths in the First World War was mainly men so that many women would not be able to find a man to marry. This surplus of unmarried women affected the common family structure. Spanish Flu almost immediately after the First World War killed large numbers of men and women so this caused a different family structure.

In Russia after the revolution in 1917, the government felt threatened and therefore women were employed in a wider range of occupations than before.

Women's education became more important after the Butler Education Act of 1944. Currently, more women are employed than men, although women are more likely to be part time than men. More men than women own cars so this sometimes limits the jobs women can obtain. However, the digital revolution sometimes means that women can work from home. Changes in the NHS and the education sector will have a disproportionate effect on women's employment since they are heavily employed in both these sectors. Childcare provision has been an aim of the current

Conservative government, the previous coalition government, and Labour party government before that. Many women however find that it is difficult to combine paid and unpaid work, sometimes called the dual burden. Sir Vince Cable (a former Liberal Democrat cabinet minister in the coalition government) has said that he wishes to see more women on the boards of the "Footsie" 100 largest companies.

The rapid speed of change

Futurist Alvin Toffler (1928-2016) discussed in his book "Future Shock" the rapid changes that he assumed would take place in society and stated his purpose of writing the book as studying how people will adjust to these changes.[25]

He made the point that some people seek change, whilst others run from it. Change means that there has to be new rules and new roles for people.

Toffler calls this a disease that he names future shock. He compares this to cultural shock, a situation in which the familiar cues are replaced by unfamiliar cues. This is often encountered in foreign travel.

He assumed that millions of people would be affected by the disorientation of future shock. The changes of the future would result in not knowing what behaviour is and is not rational given the changes in society.

Toffler discussed some of the innovations and changes that have taken place in history such as in agriculture and the effects they have had.

The book was later made into a documentary in 1972 starring Orson Wells a well-known actor, stating that the rapid rate of change was causing the age to be one of both stress and anxiety.

The book was written not long before the OPEC price changes in 1973 changed much of Western society. It caused unemployment in many countries and led to political upheavals.

There were similar shocks following the unexpected price decreases of oil in 2015.

---

23 [Dr Pamela Cox (pres.), "Shop girls: The true story of life behind the counter – 1 Here Come the Girls", BBC Two, 24th June 2014, http://www.bbc.co.uk/programmes/b0485fz3]
24 Ibid.
25 [Alvin Toffler, "Future Shock", Random House, NY, 1970, ISBN: 978-0-394-42586-3]

Chapter 9   Mass media

Mass media is a large and increasing aspect of our society today. It provides us with instant communication wherever we are and gives us access to instant news.

The mass media for most of the 20th century included newspapers, magazines, cinema and radio.

After the Second World War, this included television. During the 21st century, the Internet has become increasingly dominant, with the number of newspapers and magazines being sold declining rapidly. The mass media is often geared to entertainment and therefore can be regarded as part of recreation.

Some sports such as darts, snooker and billiards have become very important because of the publicity they get through television coverage. Even more traditional sports such as soccer, has been altered from generally having one fixture for all clubs in the same division at the same time on Saturdays to having fixtures at different times on Saturdays as well as Sunday football and sometimes a Monday, so that it is available to football fans at many different times of the week.

The amount of money that Sky and BT put into the Premier division has meant that the wages paid to the top players is extremely large. The mass media has always influenced the type of music and dancing, which takes place, but the digital revolution has meant that new music styles can be shown to large audiences much more quickly than before.

The death of Michael Jackson the pop singer in 2009 would have caused sorrow to many people, irrespective of where they lived.

The Rolling Stones (a well-known British pop group) performance in Havana, Cuba, in March 2016, would have been seen by many people across the world and not just the estimated 500,000 people who attended the free pop concert. In the 1960s and 70s, the Cuban government would not have wished people to see them because they were part of a decadent capitalist lifestyle.

Negative and positive stereotyping

The mass media can create impressions of different groups, which can be positive or negative. The phrase heroes will often be used when it is referring to the Armed Forces of the side that we are supporting. The negative stereotypes can also be seen both in the past, and currently. Jewish people in the 1930s were often stereotyped as being solely motivated by money. We now see Muslims being portrayed as the group in society most likely to be hostile to our way of life. We can see even more negative stereotyping about immigrants. However, negative stereotyping is not confined to one racial group. It can often be found in the ways that the national media will portray young people. Very rarely do the young people who may be carers hit the headlines, whereas those who go out binge drinking will be much more likely to be noticed. Similarly, older people will often be portrayed as benign, but stupid.

If you read local newspapers, you will probably find reports on how well young people have done at school and helping society as a whole. Readers are much less likely to find this in the national media. The Glasgow media group is an important source of information about the bias of the national media and their website is very helpful to students.[26]

Stereotyping of women

The mass media can create stereotype images of women as sex objects and there are currently concerns that girls as young as seven indulge in excessive dieting to conform to this image. Bulimia is therefore often a self-made disease, which occurs as a result.

Women were rarely shown as heroes in adventure films or shows, but this is gradually declining, although not as quickly as most feminists would wish.

Stereotyping of disabled people

The para-Olympics, held in the UK in 2012, and in Brazil in 2016 and widely shown across the world, may have altered the perceptions of what disabled people could do.

The mass media and sports

Sporting events have been widely publicised and this is not new. The Berlin Olympics of 1936 were used by the Nazi government as a form of propaganda. The Nazis believed in the supremacy of the Aryan race (and were disconcerted when Jesse Owens, a black athlete won several events). The term "Aryan race" was often used during the late 19th century to the middle of the 20th century to describe the idea that this racial grouping had developed many languages and was a distinct part of the Caucasian race. The Aryan race was assumed in this theory to be of European as well as Western Asian Heritage. The Nazis assumed that the Aryans were a master race and that others were inferior. Whilst the Nazis were eventually defeated in 1945, similar language has been used by the mass media currently, when looking at mass migration.

Mass media and sport in the 21st century

There has been considerable controversy about how major sporting events have been allocated to different countries. In particular, there has been widespread concern about Qatar hosting the 2022 football World Cup.

There have been concerns about the extent of doping in athletics, tennis, and other sports. There have also been concerns about gambling where sportspeople have sometimes deliberately lost so that gamblers make more money.

The mass media and political power

The mass media is also an important source of information, and control over the media is therefore important. This can readily be shown by the ways that if there is a revolution that the revolutionaries will try to take over the radio and television stations.

The growth of the newspaper market and the current decline

The newspapers have their origins in some of the newssheets that were published in the 18th century.

These had increasing circulations in the 19th century partly because of the increase in literacy, which meant there were more potential readers, and also partly because of the development of the railway system which meant that newspapers could be delivered to most parts of the United Kingdom within a day.

In the United Kingdom, the term press barons were often used and Lord Beaverbrook developed the Daily Express and Sunday Express mainly to be used as a form of propaganda. The relationship between government and the mass media has not always been very good and Stanley Baldwin (a Conservative Prime Minister) memorably described newspapers as "having power without responsibility – the prerogative of the harlot throughout the ages". Lord Northcliffe is associated with the Daily Mail. Lord Conrad Black ran the Telegraph Empire from 1985 until 2004, when he was prosecuted for fraud and subsequently jailed. Rupert Murdoch (an Australian with American citizenship) has dominated the newspaper empire.

Private eye, a UK satirical magazine, has often commented about the ways that the Murdoch empire will comment adversely about the BBC and the TV licence. Readers of the Murdoch press may be unaware that the typical subscription for Sky is much higher than the BBC licence, but this is not mentioned.

The Telegraph group was responsible for investigating the expenses scandal concerning many MPs and Lords in 2009. Apart from adding to the cynicism about politics generally in the UK, it was quite courageous since it showed the problems both in the

Labour Party, which might have been expected from a right-wing newspaper, but also problems in the Conservative party.

The relationship between the mass media owners and the government has sometimes been fraught and the Levenson enquiry showed some of the abuses of the mass media. There have been concerns about invasions of people's privacy particularly following the allegations about phone hacking especially of a murdered child.

Sociologists have often distinguished between the broadsheets (such as the Daily Telegraph, the Times, the Independent now renamed the I, the Guardian and the Financial Times) and the tabloid newspapers – sometimes referred to as 'lowbrow papers' – such as the Sun and the Mirror. Most western countries have daily national newspapers apart from the United States of America.

In 2016 the claims of the Sun newspaper, which in 1989, had claimed after the Hillsborough disaster that fans had urinated on the police and others trying to help Liverpool fans was shown to be completely false.

Radio and television

In the United Kingdom, the British Broadcasting Corporation more often known by its initials BBC, was the only organisation allowed to broadcast until In 1957, ITV came into existence and then subsequently Channel 4. The influence of satellites and digital television means that many people have a wide range of potential programs available to watch. The commercial television networks gain their revenue through advertising although there are limits on the amount of advertising per hour applying to most of the commercial television network. The TV networks have included sports channels, and the networks especially Sky and BT have often competed on their coverage of the big football matches. The amount of time watching television is considerable. Professor Anthony Giddens of the London School of Economics in the first edition of his book "Sociology" made the point that, by the age of 18, the average child will have spent more time watching television than any other activity apart from sleep.[27]

The mass media is often reliant on advertising and therefore they will usually be reluctant to annoy potential advertisers.

Whilst mass media includes, newspapers radio and television, the new social media have considerable importance. This can be shown in a simple way when people now use the phrase "to Google" when looking up information.

It has been estimated that about 95% of girls and 90% of boys in the 12 to 15 age group belonged to at least one social networking site. The figures for 7 to 11-year-olds are slightly lower with around 70% of girls and 56% of boys belonging to at least one social networking site.

Data about mass media can be obtained gained from number of different sources, especially "Measuring National Well-being". Television has been one of the most important influences on mass media, and typical United Kingdom television viewing has remained around 20 hours per week, irrespective of age and gender. In recent years, however, a number of differences have occurred: there is now a far wider variety of channels than in the past, although BBC1, ITV and Channel 4 are still the most watched channels, even allowing for online catch-up services.

TV and its educational role

Television can act in a formal educational role as with programs such as Coast where the BBC uses the Open University to not only show the coastline, but also often to give a historical background to the way in which it has changed to alter people's lives. This has sometimes been tragic, as the number of shipwrecks will show, but has also sometimes been positive, as the coast has been used to provide employment.

Sometimes television acts in an informal educational way as celebrating David Attenborough's 90th birthday in May 2016 shows. David Attenborough's nature programmes are entertaining, but will also help people to understand the ways in which animals and plants adapt to changing conditions. These changing conditions can include ways in which extensive farming and logging has changed many areas. They will also show the ways in which animals and plants are being altered with climate change. Improvements in technology means that scientists can often show in real time what is happening to people, animals, forest and fauna.

Increasing use of social media

In addition, however, to television viewing, many people will now also use the various social media networks such as Facebook, Twitter, Flickr, and so on.

Social media can be used for good purposes, such as alerting people to problems across the world and encouraging people to use information from charities and to give to them so that they can help alleviate the problems.

It can, however, also be used for bad purposes and bullying using social media is a very common occurrence. Sexting which means sending sexual images by text has become common.

Harassment, particularly of female reporters, is also common.

Explicit and implicit advertising

The mass media can often influence people, partly through both explicit advertising on the commercial channels, but also the implicit advertising on many programs which suggest that having a better house, or better car are extremely important. Whilst the number of people reading newspapers has declined rapidly and this is likely to decline even more with the decision in 2016 to have no future edition of the Independent or the Independent on Sunday, except in the digitalised version, the newspapers still exert influence on voting behaviour as well, as on a variety of different attitudes. The "i" newspaper which is much smaller than the broadsheets and which therefore summarises information more succinctly has however continued.

Surprisingly, on February 29th 2016, the owners of the Daily Mirror and the Sunday Mirror brought out a new daily newspaper entitled "the New Day". Whilst the Daily Mirror and the Sunday Mirror have nearly always supported the Labour Party, the publishers stated that it would not automatically follow this stance. However, the newspaper was the shortest lived of any national paper in UK history and the last edition was on 6th May 2016, so that it had lasted a mere nine weeks. Whilst the newspaper had originally been published with a headline figure of 20p, this had been insufficient to gain sufficient circulation. One possible reason was that it did not have enough articles to interest the serious reader, compared with the "i" which had around twice as many.

Mass media and their influence on the political agenda

Sociologists can see influence of the newspapers with the emphasis on immigration, and also on the ways in which some events will hit the headlines, even if comparatively unimportant whilst others such as the widespread massacres in some African countries such as Rwanda hardly in the headlines.

It is not however just the television and social media which can influence people, we now have 24 hours' coverage, of events, and this may come from the mass media can also come from individuals. Viewers can gain information from Syria, even whilst mass bombing is taking place from whatever different quarters.

In the general elections in the UK and many other countries, the mass media can be an important influence. After the 1992 general election where many people were sure that the Labour Party would gain control after 13 years of Tory rule, the Sun published an article suggesting it is the "Sun wot won it".

Rupert Murdoch, the chairman of the media group that controls the Sun, the Sun on Sunday, the Times, the Sunday Times and Sky television, has considerable influence on the ways that people think.

Opinion polls published by newspapers and other organisations can influence the ways in which people vote. However, whilst most responsible organisations carrying out opinion polls, will suggest that they are accurate to plus or -3%, these qualifications are not always take into account by the people reading them. The Conservative outright victory 2015 when most people had predicted another hung parliament is an example where people will have been influenced in their voting approach by the predictions. (The term "hung Parliament" is used when no one party has enough seats to form a government on its own.)

The mass media had been widely used before the local elections in 2016. In particular, the new London Mayor Sadiq Khan who is a Muslim had been portrayed by the right-wing newspapers as being a friend of Muslim extremists. The mass media whatever their views contrasted his background as being the son of an immigrant Pakistani who had been a bus driver for 25 years in London with that of Zac Goldsmith whose father was a billionaire.

Who decides what to watch on television?

Within the home, there has often been a patriarchal arrangement where what the males have decided what the family should watch. It remains to be seen whether the number of ways in which programs can be viewed including catch up or computers where the distinction between computers and television is less clear-cut alter these patterns.

Mass Media

An important part of the sociology exams is the influence of the mass media. Data about mass media can be obtained gained from number of different sources, especially Social Trends. Television has been one of the most important influences on mass media and typical United Kingdom television viewing has remained around 20 hours per week, irrespective of age and gender. In recent years, however, a number of differences have occurred, there are now far wider variety of channels them in the past although in spite of this, BBC1, ITV and Channel 4 are still the most watched programmes, even if we allow for catch up.

In addition, however, to television viewing, many people will now also use the various networking media such as Facebook, Twitter, Flickr, and so on. The mass media can often influence people, partly through explicit advertising on the commercial channels, but also the implicit advertising on many programs which suggest that having a better house or car is extremely important. Whilst the number of people reading newspapers has declined rapidly and this is likely to decline even more with the decision in 2016 to have no future edition of the Independent for the Independent on Sunday, except in the digitalised version, the newspapers still exert influence on voting behaviour as well, as on a variety of different attitudes. We can see this particularly with the emphasis on immigration, and also on the ways in which some events will hit the headlines, even if comparatively unimportant whilst others such as the widespread massacres in some African countries such as Rwanda were hardly in the headlines.

It is not however just the television and social media which can influence people, we now have 24 hours' coverage, of events, and this may come from the mass media can also come from individuals. For example, we can gain information from Syria, even whilst mass bombing is taking place from whatever different quarters. In the general elections in the UK and many other countries, the mass media can be an important influence. After the 1992 general election where many people were sure that the Labour Party would gain control after 13 years of Tory rule, the Sun published an article suggesting it is the "Sun wot won it".

Rupert Murdoch, the chairman of the media group that controls the Sun, the Sun on Sunday, the Times, the Sunday Times and Sky television, has considerable influence on the ways that people think.

Opinion polls published by newspapers and other organisations can influence the ways in which people vote. Most responsible organisations carrying out opinion polls, will suggest that they are accurate to plus or -3%. These qualifications are not always take into account by the people reading them. The Conservative outright victory in 2015 when most people had predicted another hung parliament is an example where people will have been influenced in their approach.

The media have still suggested the stereotypes in spite of feminism, we can see this for example in the ways that the clothes that women wear will be subject to scrutiny, whereas this would not generally be true of male sportsmen. However, the 1950s concept that women should simply prepare the food for the husband as he comes home tired from work is extremely unlikely to be accepted by women audiences today.

The mass media will pay considerable attention to entertainments especially BAFTA awards and Grammies. However, the 88th Academy Awards in February 2016 were heavily criticised as being white only.

Sir Lenny Henry the well-known comedian has complained that there are few black people on television.

Older women in particular have also complained about the lack of numbers of older women who are seen in a positive role. Joan Bakewell has been an exception to this. She has referred to herself cryptically as the thinking man's crumpet.

We can see that some men's magazines are almost entirely devoted to regarding women as sex objects.

Feminists, however, have also commented about page 3 of the Sun. In Ireland, Feminists have succeeded in removing the equivalent from the Irish equivalent.

Power

Who has the power in modern democracies? In the United Kingdom, we can see that in the House of Commons, there are far more men than women, and so far, only two women, Margaret Thatcher and Theresa May, have become Prime Ministers.

Apart from them, no woman has been leader of the Labour Party, the Conservative party or the Liberal Democrats or its predecessors. It can be argued that the mass media have been male dominated and that they have often tried to portray women as either too timid or too bitchy to be suitable for high office.

In the USA in November 2016, Hillary Clinton had tried very hard to become president of the USA but failed to do so.

Self-examination questions

Q1. Why have the sales of newspapers declined in recent years? Why would this be of interest to sociologists?

Q2. Why might the different newspapers reflect the proprietor's political views and why is this important to sociologists?

Q3. Why are local newspapers, a source of interest to sociologists and what data if any do they contain, which would be more difficult to obtain from other sources?

Q4. In the Second World War (1939 to 1945), The BBC gained a reputation for impartial reporting, which was unusual in such times. Why might it be very difficult to get impartial reporting from war zones?

Q5. Some people have suggested that the digital revolution makes it easier for new people to enter the industry, whilst others suggest that it makes it even easier for large corporations such as Sky and BT to be even more dominant. How would you assess the truth of this?

Q6. Why might the national media wish to portray certain groups in a positive way, but other groups in a negative way? Why might this be of importance to sociologists?

Q7. Why has the introduction of the social media made it more difficult for governments to control what their citizens, especially younger ones, watch?

Q8. What tensions are there, for much of the mass media, between relying on advertising for a considerable part of their revenue and being able to give impartial information to the public?

Q9. Why is control of the mass media a very important topic? Why have some sociologists suggested in the light of hacking scandals that we need more government control to prevent this? Why may it be difficult to get broad agreement on this?

Q10. The newspaper "the New Day" was introduced in 2016 at a lower price than its rivals. Why would it do this? What other factors apart from price would be necessary to ensure that readers bought the newspaper?

Q11. Why might sociologists be interested in the growing importance of social media?

Q12. How can interest groups use the social media to present their arguments? How for example can Oxfam use the Internet to try to influence people's opinions?

Q13. In 2016, with the referendum on whether the United Kingdom should remain in the European Union, there were many comments that the mass media presented arguments mainly about migration rather than the economic and social effects of the decision. How and why can the mass media do this?

Q14. There have been considerable debates about the future of the BBC and how far it should compete with ITV. Why might this be of interest to sociologists?

---

26 Glasgow Media Group, 2016, http://www.glasgowmediagroup.org/
27 Anthony Giddens, *Sociology* (London: Macmillan, 1989) ISBN 978-0-333-42739-2

Chapter 10   Politics and voting behaviour

Participation in a democracy can be through voting, there has been a decline in the number of people voting, although this varies between different age groups. Research from Prof Tony Travers, a well-known psephologist at the London School of Economics shows the extent of the decline in voting behaviour as well as changes in voting behaviour.

Younger people are less inclined to vote. Older people are more inclined to vote and the details about this can be found on the different political party's websites as well as from government publications.

Postal voting may make some difference to this. It is much easier now to obtain postal votes than in the past although there have been some concerns that in some cases fraud has taken place. This has particularly occurred where one person sometimes from a political party has succeeded in obtaining a large number of votes from a single household.

Some people have suggested that there should be weekend voting as in other countries. This would make it easier for many people to get to the polling stations. However, people standing for elections as members of a political party are often able to arrange lifts for people who do not have access to a car. Currently voting in person at elections takes place between the hours of 7 a.m. and 10 p.m.

People may protest as a sign of interest; we can see examples of this in 2016 with the demonstrations by the junior doctors over the pay and work conditions imposed upon them by the British government.

If the two main parties overlap in their views, then people may be less inclined to vote. Political commentators have often distinguished between left-wing parties, which will include socialist parties in most countries, and right-wing parties, which would include the Conservatives in this country but which in other European countries would be called Christian Democrats.

Sir Edward Heath, a former Conservative Prime Minister, stated once that he found Tony Blair, the former Labour Prime Minister, to be to the right of him on many issues.

The number of people belonging to the political parties has gone down, but Jeremy Corbin's leadership of the Labour Party has led to an increase in numbers of people joining the Labour Party when he unexpectedly became leader in 2015 and was re-elected in 2016.

There is a correlation between class and willingness to vote. Generally, the middle classes have a much higher turnout at all elections, whether for Parliament, the European Parliament or local elections, than the working class.

Black people vote in a different way to white people. They have been much more likely to vote for the Labour Party than for the Conservative party even where their incomes are similar.

The media influence on voting behaviour

The UK press is mainly right-wing with the Times, the Sunday Times owned by Rupert Murdoch, usually supporting the Conservative party. Similarly, the Daily Telegraph and Sunday Telegraph will also support the Conservative party. The Sunday Mirror and the Daily Mirror on the other hand, usually support the Labour party. The Guardian is more independent in its views but has usually supported either the Labour party or the Liberal Democrats. What is not clear is whether people who read the right-wing or left-wing press do so because of the political coverage or whether the coverage influences the people to vote in particular way.

Pressure groups, such as Greenpeace and friends of the Earth, will try to influence people to take more interest in climate change and to vote for candidates who are more likely to vote for environmental measures.

The press apart from the direct influence on voting behaviour may well be able to encourage particular topics to become the focus of attention. In 2016 in the run-up to the referendum on the UK continuing to be part of the European Union, or alternatively to leave it, the press was trying to influence the decision, particularly by focusing on issues such as migration.

In March 2016, the Sun newspaper tried to involve the monarch, Queen Elizabeth II, by suggesting that she had expressed views hostile to the European Union, and therefore, in turn, favour a British exit.

Voting in local elections

The voting turnout in local elections is often very low. This is disappointing, since local authorities have control of social services, which are important to the elderly and to younger vulnerable people. Whilst many schools have become academies, local authorities still control a number of different schools. The importance of local government was revealed in the considerable coverage given to the abuse-in-care of many vulnerable young women in the Rotherham area of Yorkshire.

Generally, turnout is higher where there is less turnover of residents coming into and leaving the area.

Characteristics of British MPs

The majority of Westminster MPs are white, male, middle or upper class and middle aged. In early 2016, MPs from fee-paying schools such as Eton were in prominent positions with David Cameron the then Prime Minister and George Osborne the then Chancellor of the Exchequer occupying the two most important roles.

In contrast, there are few young MPs. There are also few from ethnic minorities or from working class backgrounds.

Women are still very much under represented. However, there are signs of change:

- The Scottish National Party (SNP) has a female leader in Nicola Sturgeon

- Plaid Cymru (the Party of Wales) is led by Leanne Wood

- Arlene Foster leads the Democratic Unionist Party (DUP) which is the biggest party in Northern Ireland

- Caroline Lucas led the Green Party of England and Wales until September 2012. (She remained the Green Party's sole MP, but was replaced as leader by Natalie Bennett.). She is now joint leader with Jonathan Bartley.

- UKIP had a female leader but only for 16 days in 2016

Chapter 11 — Socialisation and culture

In sociology, we aim to look at society's common values and at the ways people behave differently to other animals.

In 2016, there have been many comments about British culture and the way that some minorities do not share the same values and have gone to join the jihadists in countries such as Syria.

Sociologists will be interested in seeing how women's position in society has changed since Victorian times.

The assumption in Victorian times was that women would not normally be expected to run businesses, or to be involved in politics at almost any level. Today we find that women have been accepted into politics although so far there has only been two women Prime Minister the late Lady Margaret Thatcher (1979 to 1990) and the current Conservative prime minister Theresa May.

Women are much more represented at all levels of business although Sir Vince Cable the former Liberal Democrat Cabinet Minister until 2015 has expressed the desire for more women to be represented on the largest companies in the UK which are often called the FTSE hundred companies.

The assumption has often been that women have much more of the parental instinct than men. There have however been exceptions when women have rejected their offspring and this has often aroused media interest although generally there has been less interest when men have taken little interest in their children.

There have been a few examples of what have sometimes been described as feral children when children have been isolated for whatever reason.

The socialisation process

Sociologists have often used the phrases primary and secondary socialisation.

Primary socialisation takes place between the individual and the group with which they are most in contact.

Children have usually been socialised within a family setting, although in 2016, there was concern about the number of children in care and what happens to them once they reached the age of 18.

Girls and boys have often been socialised in different ways. It has been suggested that, because of the future pattern of jobs, women should be taught from an early age about qualities that will help them to obtain engineering jobs, where there are still vacancies in spite of high rates of unemployment.

The peer group is also important to many children and this influence can be for good or for bad. Sociologists have been particularly interested in the gang culture and there have been many comments about this in the UK but also across Europe in 2016.

Girls have often been given dolls, whereas boys have often been given Lego or other construction toys. Not all sociologists have assumed that men and women have the same aspirations.

On the positive side, most children who play together get helpful role models and many schools try to ensure that children who are new to the school are not left out. Some schools will therefore have a buddy system.

The socialisation may take place through leisure pursuits, many people in Leicester in 2016 following their unexpected success in the Premier league will have come together not just to watch the matches but also in celebrations immediately after the match.

Many people from the middle and upper classes watch classical music, ballet, opera whereas this would be less true for the working class.

Working class people are more likely to watch greyhound racing, and this may be a popular place to meet.

Not all forms of socialisation are class-based. A large number of people mainly men are involved in the so-called heritage railways, where usually they will be recreating many of the steam railways on lines which had been closed following the Beeching report in 1963.

The activities here may include "the glamorous activities such as driving the engine" even though at the period when the railway lines were being closed British railways had had problems in obtaining staff for such jobs. It will also however use staff with many different skills such as those involved with maintenance of locomotives and rolling stock as well as providing refreshments.

Currently theatres are trying to involve working class people in the UK not just to come to theatres during the pantomime season but at other times of the year as well. Some theatres are trying to be proactive and going into schools and colleges to encourage people to watch plays and to encourage more students to take up drama. Taking part in plays whether on the stage or behind the scenes helps people to come together. It can involve a range of skills such as carpentry for helping to construct the sets, as well as providing musical accompaniments.

Public houses have always been places where the communities can come together although there have often been strong class divides.

Historically some of them would have had sawdust on the floors and although sawdust is no longer used, the same class distinctions prevail.

Whilst some public houses simply have large television sets so that people can watch sports events etc., other public houses will have groups appearing which is likely to bring people together.

Some pubs will also have quiz nights that may cater for people across the age range and class whereas others will be much more likely to appeal to a particular group of people.

Pop concerts are more likely to appeal generally to younger working class people but can help to unite communities. However, some festivals such as the Glastonbury Festival in Somerset will have much wider potential audiences and the costs of attending them will usually mean that it is the richer classes who can attend rather than the poorer.

Socialisation may also take place through work activities, with some employers traditionally having works outings, although currently the socialisation may take place through talent contests or sometimes through shows where people might sing, dance, or play the spoons.

Socialisation can also take place through living in particular areas so that people in the East End of London would generally have had a very different approach to life to those living in the Western areas of London.

Until the early 1960s, sociologists would have observed that many houses in London around Notting Hill would have suffered from Peter Rachman, a notorious landlord, whereas people in other parts of Kensington would have had very high standard of living generally but would have been unlikely to have mixed with each other. Sociologists can still find very different living styles within a very short area.

Secondary socialisation takes place within schools and many students will have to follow the national curriculum. Apart from the formal learning, there is also a hidden curriculum so that students recognise both the formal and informal hierarchy within schools. This socialisation may continue after the school years with many schools having sports societies and others which old pupils can belong to.

Whilst the Equality act 2010 in the United Kingdom aims to promote equality and therefore equal opportunities, we can see that in many primary schools that there are few male teachers and therefore students will observe this. The need for male role models has been emphasised by different sociological schools.

The mass media is extremely important in the United Kingdom, and the ways the media depict events such as migration from Syria will influence how children treat people from other backgrounds. It will also influence how boys and girls treat each other. The mass media is often accused of sexism for describing sportswomen and female celebrities in terms of their attractiveness rather than their prowess.

The social media have become a major player; women have complained about the ways in which Trolls have harassed women who have spoken out on particular issues.

Religion has also played an important part in the socialisation although church numbers have declined in recent years. When the then Prime Minister, David Cameron described the UK as a Christian society. The 10 Commandments found in Exodus 20 are common to the Abrahamic religions: Christian Jewish and Muslim people would agree that they form a moral code, which most would agree with, even if not all adhere to them.

There is a difference between recent immigrants and the rest of society. A greater proportion of those from Eastern Europe especially the Polish will have a Roman Catholic background whilst many from the Indian subcontinent may have a Hindu or Muslim background.

Differences in the socialisation process

There are differences between the different classes. The upper classes are more likely to send their children to public schools (the somewhat misleading name for fee-paying private schools in the United Kingdom).

These are the ideas within society, which can be transmitted from one generation to another. Sometimes they will be written down, but are more often passed on by speech.

There may also however be a series of sub cultures, so that youth subculture is often regarded as different to that of different generations. Sociologists can see evidence of this in some opinion polls that show differences in attitudes, for example, to same sex marriages between older and younger people.

Some cultures may also reject the main cultures of society. Some groups such as the Amish in the USA who will live in a very different manner to the rest of society. Similarly, some ultra-Orthodox Jews will have very different views to the rest of the society in which they live. Sociologists can observe the tensions that this causes in Israel and the occupied territory.

Roles

In different roles, society often expects different attitudes. We expect nurses and doctors to be concerned about our welfare. We expect teachers to be knowledgeable about the subjects and to be able to present material in an intelligent way.

Role conflicts

Role conflicts are often difficult to deal with, particularly in a small village. Being a parent may conflict with the role of being a teacher, and giving time to voluntary organisations might not allow enough time for everything else.

Status

Status is important to many people, some jobs have high status, such as being a hospital consultant, whereas others such as being a lorry bin driver will have much less status.

Sometimes status will be achieved because of a person's efforts. Most people will be aware of a particular teacher who has been regarded with affection because of the amount of effort they have put into the job and the empathy with which they have done this.

In modern British society, entertainers and sports men and women will often have very high status, which they can sometimes exploit by endorsing particular products or services.

In some societies, status may be acquired through possessions. Advertisers often emphasise this in the way that they will say that certain brands of clothes or shoes will give us status. If you watch commercial television, you will see the ways in which private vehicles are sold because of safety, which might reasonably be thought to be important, but on the ways in people owning such vehicles will be regarded. Estate agents will often label houses which they are selling as being exclusive, although it is not clear, who they are trying to exclude.

Socialisation may also be unhelpful when children are brought up in dysfunctional families such as those who are over reliant on alcohol or drugs especially if the family moves around frequently and so the families are predominately the main source of culture for the children and other agencies are far less important.

It can also be unhelpful when there is a trend for violence in one generation to spill over into other generations.

Self-examination questions

Q1. Is it true that the family will be the main influence on socialisation for most people in the United Kingdom?

Q2. If the child were bought into a dysfunctional family, such as those where the parents are alcoholics or drug addicts, would it be sensible to remove them from the child?

Q3. Some sociologists would suggest that the right approach to socialisation is that children should automatically accept orders from those in authority, such as teachers, parents, doctors. What problems if any would arise from keeping to such viewpoints?

Q4. In 2016, there were many allegations about high profile sports men and women as well, as administrators. There were also accusations about FIFA and football managers Why might this be important if young people see such people as role models?

Q5. What is meant by role conflicts and role tensions?

Q6. Why might social media be important in changing people's views about the roles that different groups play?

Q7. How can advertisers try to manipulate the ways that people perceive themselves and other groups? Explain with reference to the car sellers.

Q8. Why might status be important to many people? In whose eyes, would it be important that they achieve this status? Why might this be important to sociologists?

Chapter 12   Poverty and the welfare state

Poverty has often been researched by sociologists especially by Karl Marx and his followers. At the end of the 19th century, many people were shocked by social surveys in York by Seerbohm Rowntree (1871 - 1954) and in London by Charles James Booth (1840 - 1916). These showed the extent of poverty even when Britain was the major power in the world and many people had taken pride in its achievements.

Sociologists have been interested in the ways poverty might persist from one generation to another within the same family.

Whilst the media have often talked about scroungers, successive surveys from the 1970s onwards suggest that where benefits are means tested that a significant number of people do not apply for the benefits. There are a number of reasons for this, one is that often the forms are complicated, which may not help people whose literacy powers are limited. Not all benefits are well publicised.

Parents and children may feel stigmatised if, they apply for free school meals.

They will also have been interested in the ways that power is usually vested in men rather than women and why this might cause social divisions.

The riots in parts of the UK in the 1980s especially Liverpool led to the former Deputy Prime Minister Lord Heseltine to suggest methods of reducing the problems. This included "operation eyesore" which tried to remove derelict buildings, in the belief that neither firms nor individuals would wish to live or work in such surroundings.

The former London Docklands Development Corporation was similarly given the powers to be able to develop areas, including being responsible initially for the Docklands Light Railway, which helped to regenerate the Docklands, which had been run down very considerably as the Port of London moved downstream, initially to Tilbury. The wharves were often unsightly, putting off both employers and employees from coming to the area.

The 2011 riots in England and Wales but not in Scotland again focused attention on the problems faced by poorer people.

The origins of the welfare state in the UK

The welfare state was partially set up by the then Liberal governments from 1906 to 1914. An example of this was national insurance, which helped to provide unemployment pay under the National Insurance Act 1911. The welfare state was set up by the Labour government from 1945 onwards, partly because of the Beveridge report published in 1942. According to this report, the welfare state was meant to help people from the cradle to the grave. Whilst Lord Beveridge was briefly a Liberal MP during the war years his main influence was probably being a mentor to Harold Wilson, who was Labour Prime Minister, four times in the 1960s and 1970s.

The right wing in the United Kingdom has suggested that the welfare state by giving universal benefits has not helped to reduce waste. Some in the New Right, therefore, suggest that we have a culture of welfare dependency that instead of seeking work people will often prefer to remain on benefits.

Currently, the NHS has come under attack because some people would suggest that private medicine and treatment being paid for by people who could afford it would be more logical. There has been waste in the NHS with the biggest one being the computerisation of all patients' records. So far this has cost several billion pounds without any effective end results. This is a criticism however not of the NHS staff, but of ministers and advisers who do not understand the problems of technology. There have however also been criticisms of treatment of patients by some NHS staff.

Similarly, however, there have also been criticisms of abuse of the frail elderly by private nursing homes.

Defenders of the welfare state would suggest that it has improved the standard of health in this country, whereas infant mortality rates were high before it was introduced. There are still, however, major differences in mortality rates between different socio-economic groups. Whilst these have been fairly well known, there are also some surprising differences, for example in March 2016, there were reports that autistic children typically lived 15 years less than other people.

In 1999, the then Labour government set a target of reducing child poverty by half by 2010. More information about child poverty can be found on the Child Poverty Action Group website.

The 2010 Equality act aims to reduce inequality due to discrimination against different groups such as on the grounds of gender, age, disabilities or ethnic group. This is important since often discrimination has led to much poorer life chances for those who are regarded as being outsiders for whatever reason.

There has been concern about fuel poverty.

Many poorer people live in badly insulated houses so that their fuel bills are relatively high compared with richer people living in similar size properties with much higher standards of insulation.

Older people who also form a significant part of the poorer people in the United Kingdom often live in private rented accommodation where the fuel bills can be very high as a proportion of total income.

There are increasingly many homeless people who are employed but where in the London area their incomes are not sufficient to be able to afford accommodation. This can readily be seen in railway stations such as Victoria in London where people will sleep because it affords some type of shelter.

The middle class will have often taken advantage of subsidies given to people installing solar panels. This would have reduced their fuel bills compared to the poorer people.

Whilst the rate of inflation, in the UK and across much of Western Europe, has fallen significantly since the credit crunch 2008 onwards, food prices have risen. Poorer people may well have to travel further to shops if they wish to take advantage of the cheap prices offered by some of the larger supermarket chains.

Little attention however has been paid to the scandal that around one third of the food in the supermarket chains is wasted in the United Kingdom. If this food were used effectively then it would often involve very little cost beyond distributing it.

The Trussell Trust has set up food banks in many areas so that poorer people on production of the right documents can get food.

How much poverty there is in a country will depend partly upon the taxation system as well as on the benefits. It will also depend upon the opportunities for people to be able to obtain jobs, as well as the wages they receive. The income tax threshold has been increased in the United Kingdom, so that it is now above £10,000 for the individual. Minimum wage legislation was bought in 1999, and there is now a national minimum wage, which has been increased by more than the rate of inflation. It has been predesignated as the "national living wage", but is still substantially lower than that recommended by the Living Wage Foundation.

It is not just the wage, but whether people can obtain jobs without expensive relocation which may be important.

Donald Trump the new American president in November 2016 has stated that he will get Americans back to work. He has however also pledged that he will get rid of Obama care, which has helped many poorer Americans to receive medical help.

Self-examination questions

Q1. What is meant by the term "welfare state"? Why might it be important for sociologists to be aware of the welfare state and how if at all it can be improved?

Q2. Many people have used the term fuel poverty and have criticised the large fuel companies for charging the poor more than the rich. Are there any cost-effective ways to reduce fuel bills?

Q3. Why might some sociologists suggest that wasting food in the supermarket chains and elsewhere could be vitally important to reducing poverty?

Q4. Surveys have suggested that the number of homeless people has risen in the UK recently. What are the problems in trying to find homeless people in the first place and how might government policies affect the number of homeless people?

Q5. How does income tax and the national minimum wage legislation affect the number of poor people?

Q6. What is meant by the term welfare dependency? Unemployment can go from one generation to another particularly in poorer areas, such as Merthyr Tydfil in South Wales, where there is little scope for employment. How can central or local government help to reduce this problem?

Q7. Why might having an organisation such as the former London Docklands Development Corporation having powers to regenerate a whole area be helpful to an area which otherwise faced a vicious circle?

Q8. Why is enforcement of legislation about discrimination important as one solution to helping overcome the problem of poverty in a country, such as the United Kingdom?

Chapter 13 — Modernisation theory

Modernisation theory tries to explain how societies can progress from traditional societies (sometimes referred to as pre-modern societies) to modern societies. It often assumes that internal factors, such as the government, the country, and the ways that the educational sector can be changed, will be important to society as a whole. It may also assume that, as with Marshall Aid given after the Second World War to Europe and other countries, that modernisation can take place.

Marshall Aid was given to many countries because, whether they had been on the Nazi side or on the other side, they had lost a great deal of housing, factories, and so on. Therefore, there was a need to have a wide scale injection of money, partly to return to an era when people were optimistic rather than pessimistic. In 2016, the president of the European Union, Donald Tusk suggested there was a need to repair and improve the infrastructure of many countries including Greece, Turkey, and other countries to which most migrants have emigrated to or attempted to emigrate. There is also a need for reconstruction of Libya.

Modernisation theory was widely accepted in the 1950s and 60s, but less so after this period. However, after 1990, it became a more common model again, though it remains controversial. Many sociologists recognise that exogenous factors can be important. For example, the credit crunch of 2008 onwards, has affected many countries directly and indirectly. Tourism is a major industry and brings in overseas currency, which can be important for infrastructure. Exogenous factors can also include terrorism, and we see the effects of this in Brussels and Paris. Tourism in Tunisia and Egypt have also been affected by this.

The book "The Stages of Economic Growth: A Non-Communist Manifesto",[28] was often used to denote the phases which Roslow assumed were important to most developing countries.

JK Galbraith the best-known liberal economist has explained in some of his books why traditional societies may be reluctant to change. Sociologists may question why the commercialisation of leisure is necessarily helpful to traditional economies. For example, local communities would have been able to swim and use simple craft using local renewable resources, which would have led to sustainable economic growth.

In contrast, large cruise ships may bring in large numbers of people, but may also cause pollution, which hinders indigenous people in the first place. Sociologists can observe examples of harmful modernisation in Australia, where pollution is threatening the coral reef, which is a major contributor to biological diversity. Deforestation, occurs in many parts of Latin America with the logging companies gaining profits in the short run, but at the expense of many people, including indigenous populations in the longer term.

The problems with Haiti were made much worse because of lack of soil to hold the earth together

Germain Djontu wrote his Ph.D. on the subject of deforestation.

The theory usually assumes that there will be greater economic growth, but assumes wrongly that this is always related to economic welfare. It would help if modernisation sociologists better understood the OECD approach to economic growth.

The OECD'S measure of welfare

Traditionally, differences in welfare or economic growth over time or between countries are calculated using easily quantifiable measures, such as GNP. However, the Organisation for Economic Co-operation and Development (OECD) set out a new qualitative approach to measuring welfare in June 1973. The OECD was established in 1961 to promote policies designed to achieve the highest sustainable economic growth in employment and rising living standards, whilst maintaining financial stability, in its member countries and to contribute to world development.

OECD approach to welfare

The OECD's approach attempts to measure changes in, for example, health, working conditions and the physical environment, since changes in such indicators are likely to affect the quality of life just as changes in real national income per head are. The OECD attempts to measure the objectives of economic growth.

Health

A rise in expenditure in cigarettes is likely to lead to a greater incidence of lung cancer and to greater health expenditure. This raises GNP in two ways: firstly, as a result of the rise in cigarette expenditure; secondly, as a result of the rise in health expenditure. In this case, the rise in health expenditure recorded by GNP is not an indicator of any improvement in health. Many people are also concerned about vaping. Sociologists would wish that people adopted a healthier lifestyle, which would require little health expenditure.

As countries, such as the United Kingdom have restricted smoking in public places, the tobacco firms have often targeted developing countries where there are fewer regulations and less awareness of the risks of lung cancer and other diseases. Action on Smoking and Health (ASH) a pressure group gives information about the effects on health in the United Kingdom.

The estimate for the UK is around 100,000 deaths per year and for the world as a whole around 6 million. It is going to be more difficult to look at figures in many poorer countries, since they do not have enough medical staff to gauge the figures.

The OECD attempts to compare health over time and between countries by considering, the probability of a healthy life, which might be gauged by studying life expectancy figures and figures that show the recorded incidence of various diseases.

Similarly, alcoholism costs many developing countries many billions of pounds. The UK government tries to reduce the effect of alcoholism by getting GPs and others to stress the problems. Sociologists can consider the differences in cultures that allow some of these ideas to be replicated when others cannot.

Employment and the quality of working life

Whilst a high level of unemployment will affect GNP, even if there is full employment, there may be "hidden unemployment" which will not directly affect GNP.

The OECD attempts to measure the availability of suitable employment: if a person unwillingly moves from a poorer country to London in order to find work, whilst any work he finds will add to GNP, it may not add to welfare as measured by the OECD because there is an absence of choice of employment.

An individual who transfers from one job to another and as a result enjoys better working conditions, but receives a lower income will, according to GNP, suffer a decline in welfare, but the OECD's measure of welfare may indicate a rise in welfare.

In the UK in 2016, we can see that many people are complaining about zero hours' contracts. Currently, workers in France are also complaining about deterioration in working conditions.

People who spend a great deal of time and money on overcrowded trains as well as overcrowded roads would probably assume that if they could find work locally, they would be better off, even if they had a slightly lower income. Sociologists need therefore to look at disposable income i.e. not just after national insurance and income tax, but also after necessary expenditure such as travel.

Any improvements in working conditions over time might be gauged by the OECD from, downward trends in working hours or from the OECD's own surveys. People used to do many things such as shelling of peas with their own home nowadays most come in tins, or frozen. Are we therefore better off? Similarly with child minding, If people are paid to be foster parents or to child mind, then it will add to GNP, but if this is done within the home by parents or guardians then it will not count towards GNP.

The problems of processed foods have been highlighted with many scandals in the United Kingdom, but even more in many poorer countries. Similarly, having bottled water, even when it is tap water will add to GNP. Bottled water adds considerably to wasting scarce resources.

Time and leisure

If people have to spend a lot of money on travel in order to get to the countryside and open spaces, any expenditure on this travel will increase GNP. However, a greater provision of parks and open spaces will increase welfare as measured by the OECD, but will reduce the amount of money spent travelling to open spaces and will reduce GNP. If we were to use St James's Park in London for a heliport this would add to GNP, but most people would assume that they were worse off as a result.

If the amount of money commuters has to spend travelling to work falls (perhaps for example, the price of petrol falls) and this money is spent on leisure activities, GNP will be unaffected. Welfare, as measured by the OECD, will rise, since there will be a greater availability of effective choices between consumption of goods and services necessary for work and consumption of leisure goods and services. A small country such as Singapore will have less access to open access than a large one. As population growth is often higher in poorer countries, access to open spaces will usually be reduced.

The physical environment

The existence of pollutants and of poor housing conditions, etc. will reduce welfare as measured by the OECD. If, the output of a factory is increased, so that air pollution is also increased, welfare (as measured by OECD) will fall, but GNP will rise. Similarly, if a house is pulled down and replaced by a worse house, GNP will rise, but welfare (as measured by OECD) will fall.

Air pollution in many poor countries is extremely bad and even in Beijing is currently very poor. The same is also true of many parts of the developing world. One of the problems for many countries is that pollution does not stop at national boundaries, so that even if the country tries hard to reduce pollution it may still suffer from pollution from overseas.

The command over goods and services

The OECD sees the existence of effective choices as very important in increasing welfare. If the range of goods and services is increased by control over monopolies and the encouragement of greater competition, this may or may not raise GNP, but will raise welfare according to the OECD.

Education

Improvements in literacy and numeracy, and in the acquisition of basic knowledge, values and skills, may not increase GNP directly, but the OECD will assume that literacy is helpful

Improvements in education may be measured by increases in education facilities (which will increase GNP)., Educational standards are difficult to measure and bullying will not be measured by GNP.

Deprivation

GNP does not measure levels of over-crowding and does not measure whether houses constructed are of a good quality or of a poor quality. Yet, over-crowding and poor housing reduce welfare. The OECD attempts to measure the extent to which over-crowding and poor housing exist, by looking at housing figures (which might show how many people live in each house and whether or not a house has running water). Census data may show this.

Modernisation theory is often related to the neoliberal model, which assumes that any obstacles to economic growth such as trade union power or resistance by workers to new working conditions are bad. However, the Bhopal disaster in 1984 in the poorest part of India should have shaken this assumption. This was the biggest industrial accident disaster although estimates of the number of people killed vary but around 3000 people died directly. More recently, the Gulf of Mexico disaster in 2010, when BP did not take sufficient precautions, shows that poor supervision of organisations is unhelpful to society as a whole. Similarly, the Fukushima disaster to the Japanese nuclear plant in 2011 showed much the same. Parts of Japan are still derelict several years after the disaster. More recently, the factory accident in the capital of Bangladesh was the biggest industrial disaster in that country's history.

Traditional religious beliefs may also hinder unfettered economic growth, but this is not necessarily bad, as the film "this changes everything" has shown.

The international community and poorer communities

The film "Trashed" starring Jeremy Irons made in 2013 shows the extent of pollution from the West, often hurting poorer people living on coastlines.

Marxist criticisms and non-Marxist views

Friedrich Engels (who was the editor of the book Das Kapital with Karl Marx 1867) was only too aware of the problems of polluted streets. Critics of the Marxists would probably suggest that some of the communist regimes in practice have been just as bad, citing examples such as Trabant cars, produced in East Germany, which caused even more problems of pollution than cars manufactured by western capitalist firms.

One of the problems with the Marxist system is that it is relatively easy to quantify outputs, particularly with steel and some other products. Therefore, before the Second World War, Stalin would rigorously implement his five-year plans. People who resisted Stalin could be executed or sent to Siberia. However, one of the problems with consumer goods is that it is more difficult to gauge their quality so that an overemphasis on quantity could be at the expense of quality. Looking just at GNP does not give any indication of whether people have a choice in influencing their governments. Many sociologists would assume that freedom to choose is an essential part of welfare.

Currently, we can see problems in many countries, including those in the so-called Arab spring who would like to be able to choose their leaders rather than having them imposed upon them.

Urbanisation and individuals

Modernists often assume that along with increasing urbanisation that the individual becomes more important, and that other groups including the family become much less important. This in turn leads to more problems especially for those who may be outside the conventional system now. This could include people with visual handicaps or those who have hearing problems. It would also include those particularly in the present time, orphans fleeing from war zones such as those in Syria. As the mass migration problem in 2016 shows, these can be very large numbers.

Self-examination questions

Q1. How far is it true that we can have economic growth only if we accept very few restrictions on business activities? Which different sociological schools of thought have different ideas on this statement?

Q2. Why might some people suggest that we need the equivalent of Marshall Aid, which was given immediately after the Second World War, now to improve the infrastructure of many countries?

Q3. Why are traditional societies often reluctant to change?

Q4. Is commercialisation of leisure pursuits necessarily helpful to either poorer or richer countries?

Q5. Why might deforestation hurt not just the country in which it takes place but also many other countries?

Q6. How far is tourism a help or hindrance to countries receiving large numbers of tourists?

Q7. What is meant by biological diversity? Explain why many sociologists would regard it as important?

Q8. Why does increased travel increase the level of gross national product but not necessarily people's welfare?

Q9. Have Marxist countries such as China and North Korea avoided the problems of pollution, which have been a feature of many Western countries?

Q10. What happens to gross national product if as in the UK there are more restrictions on advertising cigarettes and other tobacco products? Does this mean that if the sales go down that economic welfare will be reduced as a result?

Q11. What obstacles are there to obtaining pure water supplies in many countries? Why might it be helpful to have international cooperation in order to achieve this?

Q12. What is meant by the term exogenous events and why are they important in the modern world?

Q13. What would happen to gross national product if we reduced the amount of land available for open access? Would most people therefore assume that if this happened that we would be better off as a result?

---

28 [W. W.2008 onwards Rostow, "The Stages of Economic Growth: A Non-Communist Manifesto", Third edition, 1991, Cambridge University, ISBN: 978-0-521-40928-5]

Chapter 14   Religion

Sociologists have studied religion for different reasons. One is that attitudes towards religion form a large part of social control in many different societies.

Sociologists have suggested that apart from religions such as Christianity, Islam, Judaism, Sikhism, Hinduism, Buddhism, Confucianism, that quasi religions such as fascism or communism have many similar effects.

Sociologists will distinguish between monotheism (the worship of one God) and polytheism (the worship of more than one God). Popular monotheistic religions worship a God who is the creator of the universe and who has laid down rules, which form a moral code for most worshippers. These rules, therefore, are extremely important, and whilst believers within a religion may have different viewpoints, they will be trying to ascertain how these rules should govern their lives.

An Example of Christianity in action

Before the introduction of the welfare state, in the United Kingdom in 1948, the Methodist Central Halls often provided many facilities for children and parents who could not normally have afforded basics such as food, clothing and health care.

Before the 1870 Education Act, Churches often provided education for children who would otherwise not have been able to afford to go to school.

Christian Aid provides help to poor people in different countries whatever their religious beliefs. It is radical (meaning it tries to get to the root of problems). In 2016, the Christian Aid website on its website mentioned the effect of climate change and that half of the world's population have lived through a disaster in the previous 10 years.

St Martin in the fields, which is very near Trafalgar Square, provides help to many homeless people.

Churches in many places often form community centres, and may have soup runs, which means that they take very basic meals to homeless people or people with very little money.

Marxists have often taken the view that religion makes life bearable; therefore, there is much less desire on the part of the working class to change. In the Marxist view, people would have religious beliefs supported by the middle and upper classes, which helps to prevent revolution. This attitude towards religion was sometimes of eternal bliss or sometimes referred to, sarcastically, as 'pie in the sky by and by'. This can lead, to what is sometimes described as an otherworldly attitude, that is, not to be concerned too much about this life since the life afterwards is so much more important. The charity Christian Aid, which spends most of its money in the poor parts of the third world, has chosen the slogan "We believe in Life before death" as a counter to this view.

It is difficult to see how Jesus telling his followers to sell their possessions and give the proceeds to the poor can be construed as a man-made religion made up by the rich. A book entitled "Rich Christians in an Age of Hunger: Moving from Affluence to Generosity" (1997) by Ronald Sider challenges the materialism of many Christians. Roman Catholic nuns take a vow committing them to poverty, chastity and obedience. The monasteries, which thrived in the UK until their dissolution by King Henry VIII in the 16th century, were also bound by similar rules, but in practice often became very rich and powerful. It is difficult to tell how rich some of the monasteries were, since Thomas Cromwell and Henry VIII were both quite capable of spinning information to suit their own ends. There were also differences between the Grey Friars and the White Friars in their attitudes towards wealth.

It is not just Christian churches who help others. The Sikh Gurdwaras in the UK have a good reputation for helping the community around them.

A national network, Christians against poverty, which was originally set up in the Bradford area organises courses to help volunteers to be able to tackle poverty on a wider basis.

Festivals and holidays affect the community as a whole. The term holiday is a word formed from holy day.

In 2016, the Conservative government was defeated on a proposal to let local authorities in England and Wales determine the hours that shops should be open on Sundays.

Not only churches objected to the proposals, but also trade unions who wanted their members to have time off.

Christmas day is a day when many shops and other retail premises are shut.

The festival of Lent is where some Christians will resolve to give up certain things they regard as unhelpful during these 40 days.

Similarly, for the Muslim community Ramadan is a period when many Muslims will not eat during daylight.

The Christian church historically objected to usury, which is where money is lent at unreasonably high levels of interest. This is one of the reasons why Shakespeare depicts Shylock (who is Jewish) in the merchant of Venice in an unfavourable light.

Whilst in the UK religious tolerance is usually taken for granted, this has not been true in the past. Jewish people were not allowed in England between 1290 when King Edward I expelled all Jews. They were finally allowed to return during the period of the Commonwealth between 1649 and 1660.

Roman Catholics were often persecuted by different monarchs, but the 1829 Roman Catholic Emancipation act allowed them not to be discriminated against.

However, Roman Catholics, particularly in Ireland still felt threatened by Protestants. This was one of the reasons for the 1916 uprising, which began at the Dublin main post office and which the First World War German government said that they would support.

The brutal suppression afterwards was one of the reasons why the Irish Free State was set up in 1922. The country is now called the Republic of Ireland.

The church and demerit goods

Many Christian churches, especially the Salvation Army have been strongly opposed to alcohol. The founder of the Salvation Army was opposed because he often saw women being violently abused by drunken men. Many men spent considerable amounts of money on drink, even if the amount of money available to other members of the family was not enough for them to live adequately.

In the USA, alcohol was completely forbidden during the Prohibition era 1922 to 1933. There are still restrictions on the sale of alcohol to younger people, although this is not rigorously enforced.

The Roman Catholic Church in particular has been strongly opposed to divorce. However, more Roman Catholics have been divorced than in the past.

The Roman Catholic Church has also been opposed, as have some other churches, to abortion. The argument is characterised by the slogans "right to life" and "freedom to choose". The 1967 act was introduced by David Steel, then a backbench Liberal MP but later leader of the Liberal Democrats. In the United Kingdom, abortion is still illegal in Northern Ireland. Northern Irish women can come to the UK mainland to have abortions, but unlike their English, Welsh, and Scottish counterparts, they must pay for the procedure, as they are ineligible for NHS treatment.[29]

Some Churches have also been opposed to homosexuality. Attitudes towards homosexuality have changed since the 1960s in the UK, although some people are still opposed.

In many African countries and some Middle East countries attitudes towards homosexuality are much less liberal and there have been cases where people have been executed for being homosexual.

Some churches have been opposed to gambling and in particular the introduction of the national lottery. They would not have wanted to see the enormous casinos the previous Labour government thought would help to regenerate cities such as Manchester.

On the more positive side, Quakers such as Rowntree established a chocolate factory in York to provide an alternative to drink. Similarly, Bourneville in Birmingham was regarded as a model village with much better working conditions than prevailed at the time.

Saltaire, near Bradford in Yorkshire, founded by Titus Salt, a textile manufacturer and Congregationalist is also a model village and had much better working conditions, as well as housing than the typical poorly built housing of the time.

Many churches formed youth clubs and had uniformed organisations such as the Boys Brigade, Scouts and Guides. These existed many years before the state had youth clubs. In November 2016, a report stated that people who had been in the Scouts or guides had better mental health than others. Religion as a problem

Many people have misused religion as an excuse to dominate other people by claiming that only they have divine truth.

Examples of this included the Crusades where Christians fought against the Muslims. We can also see this during both the Reformation and the counterreformation periods in the 15th and 16th century. We can see it more recently in the problems in Northern Ireland with violent clashes between the Protestant and Catholic factions. We can also see it in a great deal of former Yugoslavia especially with the massacre in Srebrenica.

Changing pattern of religious beliefs in the United Kingdom

In the United Kingdom, there have been an increasing number of Muslims coming particularly from Pakistan and Bangladesh but also from other countries. Similarly, there have been an increasing number of Hindus from India.

New waves of immigrants have come from Eastern Europe and have helped to increase the number of Roman Catholics.

Within the United Kingdom, far fewer people now attend church than in previous generations, although there are now variations in the membership of the different religions.

Sociologists have used the word secularisation to denote the reduction of the influence of organised religion.

Marxist view of religion

Karl Marx used the phrase "religion is the Opium of the people" suggesting that the rich used religion to control the poor even if they themselves did not obey the rules laid down, for example in the Bible.

The phrase "God bless the squire and his relations and keep us in our proper stations" was a common one in Victorian society and was used by the author Charles Dickens. This meant that God had ordered the social structure in which people found themselves.

Several school academies are owned by trusts, which put forward fundamentalist ideas. The term "Christian fundamentalist" is used to mean people who believe that the Bible is literally true.

There has been discussion about why people want their children to attend faith schools. Some will want the children to know more about their religious faith and therefore believe that the education in a faith school will help to complement what they already know.

Some of the faith schools have a better standard of education, measured by examination results compared with non-faith schools with students from similar backgrounds.

Parents may feel that faith schools provide a strong moral background, which in an era when they regard many ideas as being amoral may help their children to be better citizens.

Critics of faith schools may suggest that in divided societies, such as Northern Ireland they accentuate the problems rather than helping them.

They would also suggest that it is better to educate children in a more diverse group than in many areas where the faith schools are predominantly middle-class.

Middle class parents have often attended a church for a short period before their children reach secondary school age, so that their children can be given a place in the faith school. Some sociologists feel that appointing staff based on their religious beliefs is detrimental to an egalitarian society.

Data about the number of people holding particular religious beliefs can be found in the 2011 census.

Religion and women

Some feminists have commented about the UK churches and their attitudes towards women. As early as the 17th century, the Society of Friends more often known as the Quakers had both a male leader (George Fox) and a female leader (Margaret Fell, sometimes known as Margaret Fox). Other nonconformist denominations were slower to allow women clergy. (The term nonconformist refers to churches that are neither Anglican nor Roman Catholic). The Anglican Church, however, had its first female bishop Libby Lane ordained in January 2015. The Roman Catholic Church, however, still does not allow women priests.

Christian attitudes towards social responsibility

The Archbishop of Canterbury, Justin Welby expressed strong reservations about the excessive rates of interest charged by Wonga. He has asked Anglican churches to help to set up, if possible, credit unions, which charge much lower rates of interest than the ordinary banks. Almost as importantly, they also will give advice to people on how to avoid debt in the first place.

In some areas, such as Murston church near Sittingbourne, it has gone further by using the local primary school to help set up the credit union and explain to children about money in the first place.

The USA and religion

Critics of the evangelicals in the United States of America, would suggest that whilst the "Poverty and Justice Bible," published by the Bible society in the UK has 2100 references to helping the poor, the Republican party in the USA has done little to try to put this into practice. The Democrats have done slightly more but President Obama whilst wanting to have a broad equivalent of the National Health Service has found himself thwarted many times. Most non-Americans have found it strange that after many mass shootings that the National Rifle Association, which opposes tighter gun controls, should get support from the evangelicals. Donald Trump the new American president gained support from many Christians but was extremely hostile to immigrants and Muslims.

Liberation theology

This term refers to people who believe that the Christian church should enable poorer people to be able to take therefore place in the society in which they live. Liberation theology has been very important in South America, where corruption has often been very important and has stopped people from being able to earn their living. In some cases, prominent members of Liberation Theology Archbishop Óscar Romero (1917 – 1980) have been assassinated. Martin Luther King was also assassinated.

Supporters of Liberation Theology have been contrasted to other parts of The Roman Catholic Hierarchy who often seemed to be on the side of the oppressors. The book "world without end" by two Methodist ministers Leslie Griffiths and Jennifer Potter highlights some of the problems. Pope Francis, who is an Argentinian has been outspoken about corruption in different countries. He is the first non-European pope and is willing to look at a variety of different issues, including climate change. He raised this issue when visiting the White House when seeing President Obama.

He has also been outspoken on immigration.

Syrian civil war and effects on society

There have been more comments about organised religion partly because Syria with its five-year long civil war has killed many Syrians but has also led to large numbers of people trying to migrate.

Claims by Isis that it has carried out what most people would regard as terrorist attacks has led to some people adopting an anti-Islamic stance. This has become increasingly true after the attacks in Paris in 2015, and in Brussels in 2016.

Paradoxically, on the same day that the attack in Brussels hit the news headlines, the former leader of Bosnia-Herzegovina, Radovan Karadzic was jailed for forty years for the Bosnian genocide. During the Bosnian war, around 8000 prisoners of war were killed in cold blood in one night, whilst they were meant to be under the protection of the United Nations, Dutch contingent.[30]

President Assad of Syria has adopted a hard line towards his opponents. Few people have apparently noticed that his ally President Putin of Russia claims to be a Christian.

Killing people, for their religious beliefs is nothing new. The Second World War saw around 6 million Jews killed in concentration camps by Nazi Germany, an extreme example usually referred to as the Holocaust.

Conflicts, even within a religion, can be severe. In January 2016, Saudi Arabia executed 47 people, it claimed were terrorists, although to most outsiders they would have been seen as protesters against a very hard line regime. The UK government was criticised for not making a protest, partly because sales of arms to Saudi Arabia were very good for some parts of UK industry.

Hypocrisy and self-righteousness are not confined to people within a religion. There has however been a danger that religious people have been more concerned about the reputation of the faction they belong to, rather than what happens to victims. There have been a number of sex scandals affecting a wide variety of different groups within both the Christian religion and others. The victims have often complained that they were not listened to. Pope Francis has made sex scandals affecting the Roman Catholic Church, one of his priorities to clear up.

Self-examination questions

Q1. Why have sociologists been interested in the ways that religion affects society?

Q2. Why is it difficult to judge whether someone really believes in a religion?

Q3. Why have faith schools have been controversial because of their divisiveness in the United Kingdom? Why might some parents choose to go to church for a few weeks before they have to decide to which school they send their child?

Q4. Why have other schools such as some Roman Catholic schools insisted that potential children's parents will have had to go to church for a long period before accepting them as genuine members of the church?

Q5. What is meant by liberation theology? Why is it important?

Q6. Since the Holocaust occurred many years ago, why are the attitudes that caused it still relevant today?

Q7. Why should the people in organised religions be concerned about climate change?

Q8. In all branches of sociology, there are often problems about getting impartial data. Why might this be even truer about religious attitudes?

---

29 [Amelia Gentleman, "Northern Irish women ask to be prosecuted for taking abortion pills", The Guardian, 23rd May 2016, https://gu.com/p/4jgxy]

30 [BBC News, "Radovan Karadzic jailed for Bosnia war Srebrenica genocide", 24th March 2016, http://www.bbc.co.uk/news/world-europe-35893804]

Chapter 15   Crime and deviance

Crime

Crime is a major problem which sociologists investigate. It is always difficult to be certain about crime figures since in most countries, reported cases of crime are not necessarily representative of the true/actual crime numbers. Instances of sexual harassment and domestic violence are rarely reported to the authorities. Even murders are generally under reported. This was shown by the case of the late Dr. Harold Shipman, a general practitioner in the UK, who was convicted of 15 murders in 2003, but who was suspected of carrying out over 200 murders. This would have made him the biggest serial killer in England.

This estimate was obtained by looking at likely death rates for patients of other general physicians and comparing it with his. He later committed suicide in Wakefield prison in 2004 after having been given a life sentence with the recommendation that he should never be free.

Usually however murders will be much more thoroughly investigated than many other crimes.

Crime and norms

When looking at crime we can see that part of it is the failure to conform to the norms of society. The majority of people will have committed some crimes at a stage in their life. Most vehicle owners will have exceeded the speed limit at some stage in their life. Currently many motorists and lorry drivers take phone calls whilst driving, Many people have stolen items including those from their office or not paid for phone calls, a large number of people have taken illegal drugs whether marijuana or cannabis and a great many people would have purchased cigarettes at an age below that which is allowed within British society. The same is true of purchasing alcohol.

What is regarded as deviant in one year era may be different from another. For example, in the 19th century taking some form of opiates would have been normal. Wars were fought by British against the Chinese to get opium imported into the United Kingdom in 1839-1842 and 1856-1860.

Similarly, what might be regarded as deviant in one society, may be different in another. In Kalahari society, marriage can occur as early as 9. Polygamy, where a boy may marry several people including sisters, is allowed. Sex however is not allowed until after puberty. This type of behaviour would be in contrast to Western society norms. It illustrates that deviance in one culture would be regarded as the norm in another.

People may well not conform to societies norms without necessarily being guilty of criminal offences. People who are adopting a hippy lifestyle are not committing a crime. This is nothing new people would have been hermits and commended for this.

Some people have decided that they don't like what they regard as the rat race and may live in a community such as those associated with Rudolf Steiner (1861 – 1925) or the Iona community which was founded by the Rev George MacLeod in 1938, which is associated with the Church of Scotland. He took people from a poor Dockland parish in Govan, Glasgow, as well as young trainee clergy who worked together to build the monastic quarters of a medieval abbey, working together as they did so. This would be regarded as deviant by many people but would not be criminal. Similarly, the Archbishop of Canterbury Justin Welby has invited some younger people to live in Lambeth Palace with a more communal style which again would be deviant but certainly not criminal.

Measures of crime

Social Trends now entitled Measuring National Well-being which can be obtained free of charge from the office for national statistics states there are 2 different measures of crime. The first is the measure of crime which is recorded by the police and comes therefore from victims of crime from recording their complaints to the police. The other includes the British Crime Survey, whereby surveys of victims are carried and others are carried out. The other point is that even within these measures there are problems, for example in 2008--2009 about 4.7 million crimes were recorded by the police some of these were due to the methods of recording crime. The British Crime Survey by contrast had suggested much higher figures that of 10.7 million crimes in 2008-9. Some crimes such as domestic abuse have been under-reported. Similarly, this is true of sexual harassment and assault. High profile trials following Operation Yewtree and the problems which Jimmy Saville (a well-known TV presenter) had caused meant that more people were likely to come forward with complaints about harassment etc. This makes it difficult to know whether the publicity causes reported crimes to rise or whether the number of crimes has actually risen. This is sometimes referred to as problems of distinguishing between causation and causality.

Unreported crimes

There are a number of reasons why crimes are not reported. The first is that often, the incident is regarded as too trivial, or the police couldn't do anything, the victims did not report the crime as it was done in private. The police themselves may not report crimes for the following reasons: they may try to avoid the paperwork involved; they may try to put people off reporting crimes or even suggest they contact other agencies. Therefore, quantitative data that suggest major increases or major decreases in crime are regarded with some degree of caution. It might also be noted that perhaps the most common crimes are those committed by motorists, for example, transgressing speed limits, and these are very unlikely to be recorded by either method.

Why some crimes are likely to be under reported

Most people would regard violent crime as perhaps most important, but reporting of such incidents may vary according to the cause. Women are far more likely to suffer domestic violence than men. Domestic violence against men may be under-recorded partly because there is often no recourse for social workers for male victims and it may seem a plausible hypothesis that the police are unlikely to take male victims seriously enough.

One major cause of the under-recording of domestic violence is that women may be unwilling to admit that the incident has taken place. It could also be that sometimes the women believe it to be an isolated incident and thus not worth reporting. Research estimates in Social Trends suggested that 1 in 4 women would experience domestic violence at some time during her life. If this is true, it would suggest, (in line with feminist thinking) that such crime should be taken more seriously. The number of deaths from domestic violence is also quite high which seems yet another reason why the investigation of such crimes and preferably measures to prevent them should be more of a priority.

Crime and punishment

Social workers and sociologists in general may have quite a lot to say about the use of prison, probation and other attitudes towards punishment. The number of people in prison in the United Kingdom has risen rapidly to over 71 000 by mid-2002 which is an increase of over 25 000 since 1990. In early 2010 records showed that around 83 000 people were in prison, this has seen a small increase to just over 85 000 for mid-2014. It is unlikely that this represents an increase of the number of crimes by this percentage and could reflect a number of different factors, such as, the tendency to give prison sentences when other measures could be used; giving slightly longer sentences or even that the police have been better at catching people in certain categories. Men much more frequently commit crimes than women and therefore there is a much higher proportion of males in prison rather than females. How far this is due to social attitudes and how far due to inherent nature of the male is very much a matter of debate.

Also, the young are much more likely to commit crimes than people of older ages. The peak age is 18 for males and 15 for females. Data shows that theft is by far the most common offence for both male and female. This again has led to much comment by sociologists about the influence at school and at home. The 'nature' versus 'nurture' debate has been one that has been widely debated by sociologists and others. Some sociologists such as Sylvia Walby suggest that men are inherently violent. There is also much debate about whether people are inherently programmed to commit crimes or perhaps commit crimes as a result of their conditioning at home or at school. Clearly there are some other factors that come into play; otherwise everyone in the same social condition would do the same things.

Sociologists may also have views about types of punishment. Evidence suggests that the young are more likely to commit crimes as well as with less educated as opposed to the old and the more educated respectively. Some people have suggested therefore that better education and in particular better education in preschool ages might well help to reduce the volume of crime. This again can be a matter of quantitative research. There has been some quantitative research into the effect of supervision orders and action plans and that research in 2000 found that there was a reduction in reconviction rates across all offence categories between 1997 and 2000.

Drugs offences and age

There has been considerable debate about the use of drugs. In particular, the use of cannabis which is usually held to be the most widely selected drug in the UK. The then Labour government in 2004 changed the drug from class B to class C which resulted in maximum penalty for possession falling. It was then changed back to a class B drug in 2009 with a later Labour government.

It is usually assumed that drug offences are more likely to be carried out in certain age groups, for example the young rather than the old. How far drug offences vary from one year to another and possibly even from one area to another may be due to the seriousness with which different police forces regard such crimes. There was considerable comment in the London area where one major policeman suggested that some drug crimes should be virtually ignored.

Ecommerce and Crime

Ecommerce is not a crime free system, the most common type of crime when purchasing online is fraud. The two most common types of fraud committed are misrepresentation of the item and non-delivery of goods after payment.

Non-delivery of goods after payment is what it sounds like. A buyer purchases a product online, pays of the item to be delivered and the product does not turn up. The next step is to contact the sender which has a chance of turning into an argument with the sender saying that buyer is lying and accuses them of fraud. EBay the popular online auction site has a money back guarantee; this means that after an investigation the buyer may get the full amount spent of both the product and the postage back.

The misrepresentation of an item is the selling of an item that is not as described. This can be seen in the case of a UK buyer who purchased on eBay what he believed to be a genuine Xbox One games console for over £400 in 2013, what he received was a picture of the console.

These crimes not only affect the buyers; they can affect the other companies as well. EBay was successfully sued in 2008 by Louis Vuitton Moet Hennessy (LVMH) in France over the sale of fake goods. The claim was that eBay was not doing enough to stop the sale of these counterfeit goods.

White-collar crimes

Sociologists and the media have often concentrated on what might be regarded as working class crimes. There have however been exceptions to this so that Edwin Sutherland 1883 to 1950 in his book 'The Professional Thief' (1937) states that white-collar crimes are very prevalent in society. This would have included bribery as well as ignoring safety laws. Bribery according to the Chartered Institute of Purchasing and Supply is extremely common with overseas contracts. There have been many examples of bribery for arms contracts and the campaign against the arms trade website highlights this. The USA and to a lesser extent the UK have spent considerable sums of money in Afghanistan and Iraq for reconstruction of those countries. This has not often helped the people at the bottom of the social ladder since the money has been siphoned off. Malala Yousafzai the courageous Pakistani young lady who was shot by the Taliban for speaking out in Pakistan against the abuses imposed by them, in her book 'I Am Malala: The Girl Who Stood Up for Education and Was Shot by the Taliban' highlights how common bribery and corruption is in Pakistani society.

In countries, such as Colombia drug smuggling is rife and the drug barons exert considerable influence. Tax evasion is very common by the large corporations and the British government and others have been put under pressure to try to reduce this. This has become much more scrutinised after the Panama revelations in April 2016.

Some of the effects of bankers actions can hardly be overestimated with manipulation of key rates of interest such as Libor which is the rate at which banks lend to each other.

Safety procedures have often been lax in both the developed and developing world. In the 1970s in the United Kingdom when a great deal of attention was paid to strikes, more days were lost by accidents than through strikes and many of these were due to both management and workers attitudes, but more often the managers.

In the United Kingdom and most other European countries tachograph regulations have been imposed which record time, distance and speed. For a long while in the United Kingdom, the regulations were resisted. The phrase 'spy in a cab' was often used. Managers together with drivers frequently flouted the hours even though safety is important.

Lack of safety provisions led to the Bhopal disaster in India 1984 which claimed around 20,000 people's lives and where the successor company Dow has still not paid adequate compensation. More recently BP was heavily criticised in 2010 for lack of interest in safety procedures which led to loss of life in the Deepwater Horizon oil spill in the Gulf of Mexico and ruined many livelihoods of local people.

Whilst many MPs and Lords have expressed hard-line views on law and order, the expense account scandal which the Daily Telegraph courageously pursued showed how many MPs and peers were willing to gain from lax supervision. Hypocrisy from law and order hardliners is not new. President Richard Nixon and Vice President Spiro Agnew had been elected on a very hard-line agenda. They resigned because of the Watergate scandal when they were spying on rivals.

Currently hacking has been a major problem pursued by several different newspapers. The trial of Andrew Coulson, former News of the World editor and Downing Street director of communications for the then Prime Minister David Cameron, shows how widespread it was.

Lack of interest in food safety and labelling has been demonstrated by the horsemeat scandal in 2013.

Game Related Violence

There are many stories that relate video games to violence. Though it is a common defence in court there is very little evidence that the violence in games relates to violence in real life. A major voice in the fight against violent video games is US lawyer Jack Thompson. He describes these games as 'Murder simulators'.

In 1999 Eric Harris and Dylan Kalgold went into their school and started shooting staff and students. This incident is referred to as the Columbine High School Massacre. It was alleged that the two students were obsessed with the popular first person shooter game Doom.

Rockstar Games who created the popular Grand Theft Auto (GTA) series have been linked to several crimes. It is because of this they have drawn attention from Jack Thompson. In 2003 there were two events that related Grand Theft Auto to the crimes. The first was that of Devin Moore whose defence team suggested that the game had inspired him to murder two police officers and a dispatcher. The other was the killing of a man and the wounding of a woman by brothers Joshua and William Buckner who told investigators that they were influenced by the game.

Which groups most harm society?

If the logic of looking at case of crime and how much crime there is, is to try to protect society against harm by individuals then it would seem logical to try to work out what the probability of some crimes taking place is and also how harmful they are. Clearly murders are one of the most harmful of crimes but fortunately such crimes are rare. Whilst road accidents are far more of a risk to the young than murders very little research seems to have been done to reduce this. In most cases, the very people who proclaim to be in favour of law and order usually ignore the problems of road accidents.

If the logic of crime prevention is to reduce risk to the individual members of society then it would seem sensible to find out first what causes harm to members of society. The Royal Statistical Society has been pressing to try to find some measures of risk which would be understood by members of the public who are not necessarily numerically literate.

The word 'accident' is a cause of bias since for a long while accident meant something that happened by chance and clearly most road accidents do not fall into this category. The risks to children from road accidents are far greater than that of abduction and other related crimes. In spite of media hyperbole, the number of children killed in the way of James Bulger (the young child killed in February 1993 by two young children about the age of 9) has varied slightly from one year to another because of the nature of the crime but has not increased or decreased significantly over the last 50 years. Perceptions of crimes are often said to be almost as important as the crimes themselves. In 2001-2002, two thirds of persons interviewed said that they believed national crime over past few years have increased a lot even though most data suggested that crime levels were falling. The media do often report any figures which seem to suggest that crimes are rising but not any which suggest crimes are falling.

Sanctions

There are a variety of different sanctions against people transgressing formal rules for example to shun or ostracise them in school or college if they do not conform. The phrase sending to Coventry means not talking to people.

Society as a whole now takes for granted that prison, particularly in the USA, is a very common sanction. Historically this was not true and most prisons would not have been able to hold very many people. Also, conditions in prison depended partly upon the wealth of the individual as richer people would have been able to have a reasonable standard of life as they could pay for food and drink to be brought into them. Punishments such as corporal punishment and executions would have been public partly because they were seen as a deterrent to others. For more minor offences putting people in the stocks where they could be ridiculed as well as having things thrown at them was seen as a method of public humiliation. Nagging women would have scolds around them which was a highly visible method of punishment.

The most important rules from the government point of view were often church related, so that blasphemy would be punishable by death. The concept of an eye for an eye and a tooth for a tooth which is in the Bible quoted by Jesus Matthew 5, verse 38 was meant to deter the idea of blood feuds whereby killing or humiliating any one person could have led to a much larger retaliation.

Modern prisons date from the 17th century when workhouses provided a job for people who might otherwise have been homeless. Robert Peel 1788 -1850 the Conservative Prime Minister abolished executions for many minor offences as well as setting up the idea of the modern police force which is why we sometimes still hear the phrase bobbies to denote a police man or women.

Elizabeth Fry 1780 - 1845 the prison reformer and Quaker tried very hard to improve the lot of prisoners and to ensure if possible that they could be trained and rehabilitated. The Howard League for penal reform is the oldest prison charity in the United Kingdom and was formed in 1866. In the 20th century Lord Longford, a Labour peer 1905-2001, tried very hard to help prisoners. He had been a politician. He was mocked by some of the media for trying to help Myra Hindley, a notorious murderess.

The phrase 'punishment fit the crime' although taken from operetta by Gilbert and Sullivan is still appropriate. It is not obvious why when a prisoner was giving birth she should have been handcuffed to a bed when her offence was not paying a TV licence. Many people would have thought that far more serious offences were committed by establishment figures, including members of parliament and Lords.

Functionalist explanations of crime

Functionalists would suggest that society as a whole is based on a value consensus. This leads to social solidarity which relies on both socialisation and social control. If there is too much crime within a society or even if people fear crime too much then it will destabilise society. Functionalists are realistic enough to realise that some crime is inevitable and this is universal across all societies. Functionalists would suggest that there are two reasons why crime exists; because not everyone is equally effectively socialised and because is a diversity of lifestyles and values.

Durkheim stated modern society there is a tendency to anomie which most people would simply call normlessness. As the division of labour becomes more specialist, and people cannot see they have any control over their work, the collective conscience of society is weakened and therefore is likely to lead to higher levels of crime.

Durkheim also suggests that there are positive functions of crime. Firstly, crime can be used as a form of boundary maintenance. This will unite members of society in condemning wrongdoers and reinforce the norms and values of society. The function of punishment is not however to make wrongdoers suffer but to reaffirm social solidarity.

Another positive function of crime is adaption and change. All changes in society occur originally with an act of deviance. There has to be some method which allows scope for challenging existing norms and values. If there is complete suppression of new ideas this will lead to a stagnant society. There needs to be a balance as too much crime will tear the bonds of society and too little will lead to repression.

Cohen adds that high levels of crime can act as a warning that society is not functioning properly.

Eriksson suggests that the real function of agencies of social control is to maintain a healthy level of crime e.g. through labelling if there is too little crime.

One of the criticisms of the Functionalist theory is that Durkheim doesn't identify a way of knowing what amount of crime is the right amount.

Just because crime does certain things doesn't indicate why crime exists.

It ignores how different functions affect different individuals or groups within society. It doesn't always provide solidarity and people can become isolated.

Subcultural explanations of crime

Deviance can be caused by a delinquent subculture that has different values to mainstream society. Subcultures provide an alternative opportunities structure mainly for the working class. People who are alienated or perhaps have been labelled in some way as failures, feel that the opportunities to become a gang leader or to be associated with people who are seen by the subcultures as successful is attractive.

Cohen suggests that because the lower classes cannot achieve mainstream goals by legitimate means people may find it attractive to achieve goals in another way. However, some people suggest that this is too focused on individual people and utilitarian crime.

There have been focuses on why working class boys face anomie while fewer girls are involved in crimes. The middle-class values in the school system can lead to cultural deprivation for lower classes. If people have frustrations about their status, then they are likely to reject the values of the middle class and form delinquent subcultures. These are often characterised by spite, malice, hostility and contempt for the mainstream. This would be in line with what Willis found about education.

This subculture functions as an alternative status hierarchy which can give status to individuals from their peers. This offers an explanation of the non-utilitarian crime, but assumes that the working class start off sharing middle-class goals only to reject them when they fail. One possibility is that the working class never accept the middle-class values so they do not regard themselves as failures.

Cloward and Ohlin suggest that not everyone adapts by innovation. There is an unequal access to legitimate and illegitimate opportunity structures. In the illegitimate opportunity structure, people still need to learn a trade which means they can still fail. Different neighbourhoods will provide different opportunities and there are therefore three different types of deviant subculture.

The first is a criminal subculture where there are 'apprenticeships' that allow younger members to associate with long-standing adult criminals. This is in line with Dickens's characterisation of Fagin which would be based on Victorian real life.

In high population areas, there is likely to be a conflict based deviant subculture. In such areas, there is no stable criminal network and so the subculture would be loosely organised and based on violence. Turf wars will release the frustrations of not succeeding in the legitimate opportunity structure.

The third subculture is that of retreat, whereby people who feel themselves to be failures in both the legitimate opportunity structure as well as the criminal structure. This route may lead go illegal drug use.

One of the criticisms of this approach is that it is deterministic and over predicts what will happen to the working class. Some argue that the subculture types may be too strict as in practice people may drift in and out different opportunity structures.

Interactionist explanations of crime and deviance

Interactionists are interested in how and why certain acts are defined as criminal. They would suggest that no act is inherently criminal and deviant in itself and needs to be looked at in all different situations at all times. It is only when others label something as such that it is deviant; the nature of the act itself doesn't make it deviant. It is society's reactions to the action that makes it so.

We can see examples of this particularly relating to drugs, alcohol and tobacco. Many societies would have taken it for granted e.g. in Victorian society, people could take opium or derivatives and Valium (now called Diazepam) which was widely used to pacify children had an opium base. Similarly, modern society takes it for granted that sexual acts are usually private, but James Cook, the first white person to discover the South Sea Islanders, noticed they were surprised about this convention.

Most people would take it for granted that we should not be violent towards other people for no obvious reason yet in the 19th century and before, people of other races could be regarded as inferior whether the so-called red Indians in what is now the United States of America or the Maori's in New Zealand. According to Becker, a deviant is someone who has been labelled as deviant but this doesn't explain why laws get made.

Becker would suggest that we need to see how the laws get made. He would be interested in moral entrepreneurs who lead crusades to change the law. Sociologists can observe that Josephine Butler (a well-known Victorian social reformer) had to fight very hard to get the age of consent for sex to be raised to 16, whereas before this period it had been taken for granted that employers and sometimes relations would have sex with younger people.

We can see examples of religious books such as the Old Testament rules about marriage. The Muslim religion allows up to 4 wives, similarly in South Africa during the apartheid regime miscegenation i.e. marriage, cohabitation or sex with somebody from a different race would have been an offence.

In a society based on land ownership trespassing can be an offence whereas in Sweden people are allowed to roam anywhere except within a very narrow distance of people's houses.

Becker argues that new laws create new groups of outsiders. We can see examples of this during the Prohibition era in the United States of America (1920 - 1933) and similarly find examples of this in some Muslim states.

Platt argues that juvenile delinquency has been created by campaigns aimed at protecting young people at risk and this was a definition which the upper-class Victorian used more than others. It established juveniles as a separate category of offenders with their own courts.

Becker would suggest that social control agencies may also campaign for changes in the law to increase their own power. He argues that it is not the harmfulness of behaviour that leads to new laws being created but the effects of powerful individuals and groups to redefine behaviour as acceptable. Particularly during the Commonwealth period in the United Kingdom 1649-1660 a range of different offences were created and it was agreed that not everyone who commits a crime gets punished. It depends on the agencies of social control, the appearance of the 'offender' and the background/circumstances of the offences.

In the United Kingdom, drink-driving in the 1970s killed far more people than all the murders put together yet was not taken seriously. The USA currently has very high level of road accidents but are not taken seriously. Piliavin and Briar suggest that decisions to arrest were based on physical factors such as manner and dress. In 2016, stop and search powers were widely criticised where black people are disproportionately targeted groups.

According to Cicourel people concentrate on certain typifications, which have resulted in a class bias, as the working class fit these typifications most closely. Other agents of social control reinforce this. Probation officers may assume that middle class people are less likely to offend and therefore are less likely to support non-custodial sentences for working class offenders rather than middle class. There are suggestions that justice is negotiable for the middle-class as their parents can negotiate on his or her behalf. Cicourel also suggests that official statistics do not give us a valid picture of the patterns of crime and should be treated as a basis for research.

Labelling theory

Lemert argues that there are two types of deviance. Primary deviance includes acts that do not get labelled, and are usually trivial, like fare-dodging. However, secondary deviance includes acts that were labelled, and often gave people 'outsider status.' This could lead to the offender having a 'master status' as an offender and an outsider, which leads them to adopting a deviant career.

Jock Young found that trying to control deviance can lead to further deviance amplification. He found that drug-use among hippies was just a peripheral part of their lifestyle until they were labelled as deviant. This led to drug-use becoming a central activity among the group. This is an example of a moral panic – where the media demonise 'folk devils' and label them as deviant, calling for more control on such groups etc, which leads to a deviance spiral. Triplett and De Haan found evidence similar to this when truancy was re-labelled as a more serious crime, which caused harsher penalties – but this did not decrease the level of truancy. This was not however inevitable. David Downes and Paul Rock suggest that people cannot predict whether deviants will have a deviant career as they have free will, and can choose not to deviate further.

Lemert also suggests that trying to control deviance often leads to an increase in the level of deviance and greater attempts to control it leads to even higher levels of crime. Cohen and moral panics suggested that society's reactions to the mods and rockers were exaggerated by the press which in turn led to unwarranted moral panics. The public concerns led to more arrests and harsher penalties. The demonising of them caused them to be marginalised.

Labelling and the criminal justice system

Attempts to control people have often had the reverse effect. Re-labelling offences as being more serious leads harsher offences sentences and a new level of violence. Therefore, the labelling theory is important in determining wide scale policy implications.

It might be suggested that we should avoid naming and shaming. This would be in contrast to some USA states where prisoners have to wear different garments to show who they are. John Brathwaite suggested that there are two types of shaming. Disintegrative shaming involves labelling both the crime and the criminal as bad, and the offender is subsequently excluded from society. However, reintegrative shaming labels the act but not the actor, avoiding stigmatising the offender, but still allows them to be aware of the impact of their actions. Braithwaite believes that this type of shaming encourages others to forgive, and argues that in such societies the crime rate is much lower.

One of the problems with dealing with the functionalist approach to crime is that there is no major theoretical perspective about crime when we compare this with the Marxist views on anomie and how the capitalist system breeds crime.

Similarly, there is no one interpretation of crime statistics or source of criminality.

However, Durkheim had suggested that in advanced societies there will be more crime because in advanced societies there will be less cohesion than in less economically developed societies. This is because there are not the same shared values across individuals.

Functionalists could suggest that this is because at harvest time for example in the 18th century all the villagers were involved in the process, almost irrespective of their age and both men and women as well, as children would have been involved in this. We can contrast this to the present day, when few people are involved in agriculture and in most cases, the division of labour means that we do not know what happens in the food chain.

Functionalists could point to the so-called horsemeat scandal in 2013 when it was clear that the supply chain was not working efficiently so that people knew what they were buying and under what conditions.

We can see offences such as to the major supermarkets selling water as spring water for inflated prices when it was just out of a tap. Food poisoning is often quite common partly because the division of labour is such that people do not see where food is being cooked so that they cannot judge for themselves what is happening. Processed foods are not bad in themselves, but make it more difficult compared for example with the 18th century when sociology was being developed when most people could see the limited amounts of fruit and vegetables and meat available, and could judge for themselves, whether it was healthy or not by visual inspection.

Durkheim stated that even if all individuals were perfect, there would still be deviance, since even the slightest slip would be regarded with horror. There would not however be murder or robbery.

Durkheim also argued that society is dysfunctional, if the rate is either extremely high or extremely low. If there is no deviance, there will be no progress. This is because deviance leads to innovation, whereas conformity will not do so. If on the other hand, there is little in the way of collective views, then the status quo will no longer hold and we will have more problems.

The public response to crime is extremely important. We can see in the 19th century that punishments for crime were usually held in public, whether this was for executions or floggings or scolds for women.

Executions were extremely popular and the public could show its opinions about the executed man by booing or cheering as the event took place.

Durkheim suggested that the function of punishment is not to remove crime but to heal the wounds done by the crimes.

The functionalists would suggest that prison generally does not work because around two thirds of the first-time jailbirds do not go back, whereas two thirds of those who do go back become recidivists.

We can see this in the words of Gilbert and Sullivan that the punishment does not fit the crime. For example, one pregnant woman was handcuffed to her bed, having committed the crime of not paying her TV licence, whereas on the other hand, some of the large banks have been guilty of manipulating LIBOR. This has vast bad social repercussions for society since it determines the rate of interest paid by mortgage holders, as well as by many other people paying interest on their loans.

The large banks as well as Northern Rock were certainly guilty of negligence and sometimes fraud, but few of them have received punishments for this.

The Co-operative bank, as well as the stores was brought down by the lack of adequate supervision by chairman the Rev Paul Flowers, a Methodist minister, as well as by other directors.

Even Nick Leeson, who single-handedly bought down Barings the bank which existed for around 200 years received a relatively minor punishment.

We can also see that large firms such as BP, with the Gulf of Mexico incident, which killed 11 people, as well as hurting several thousands of people's livelihoods were not adequately punished for this and the BP chairman walked away.

The assumption of stakeholders and functionalism is that we are all in it together to use the current jargon, whereas Dow, which was the company, which owns the organisation, which killed several thousand people in Bhopal in India in 1984, has still not paid any great amount of compensation.

We can see more recently that Mitsubishi the car company has admitted fiddling the figures since the early 1990s. There is likely to be compensation but unlikely that the chairman will personally receive any great punishment. Figures about carbon emissions and therefore about climate change have been falsified, which will have large-scale effects on society, not just in the UK but across the whole world. Currently we can see that the former chairman of British Home Stores, who was advising the government on efficiency has walked away from that company, which may mean the loss of 11,000 jobs without forgoing money even though he sold the company for £1 to an organisation with no great financial skills and no record of dealing with the clothing industry.

People have however criticised Durkheim's views since it doesn't explain why some groups have much stronger forms of deviance than others.

A fragmented society in which some people feel they are the outsiders might be expected to have stronger forms of deviance and possibly more crime, if people do not feel that they are part of the society to which they are meant.

Some would suggest that if as evidence shows people have similar aspirations that if people do not achieve these aspirations in the normal way, then they are likely to seek alternative routes to success, which could be through belonging to gangs which give esteem.

In Sicily in Palermo, the Mafia run the whole port.

We can also see that where there is a breakdown of society such as in Libya that where there is no overall control of that country that it is much easier for crimes to take place, then where there is a single unified government.

Similarly, in Iraq, we can see that a great deal of corruption has taken place and that little has been done to prevent this, as was shown by the many demonstrations.

We might also notice that the norms of society may differ across different eras.

Drinking too much would have been normal in the 18th century where the phrase drunk for a penny, dead drunk for tuppence would have been common. Before John and Charles Wesley set up the Methodist church, drinking by men was assumed to be the norm. The number of gin palaces in London was huge.

Similarly, this often led to violence against women which was often taken for granted.

Currently some areas have alcohol restrictions and that there are restrictions on carrying alcohol on some trains, especially to football matches and some other sporting events.

in the USA,In the prohibition era, far more crimes about alcohol would have taken place.

There are always disputes about demerit goods which will vary from one society to another, but they would include alcohol, tobacco, drugs, including cannabis, and any other addictive substances. At the moment, there are disputes about so-called legal highs.

Again, functionalists might argue that there is no obvious logic, for example, cigarettes kill around 100,000 people per year, whereas ecstasy probably kills around 10 people per year.

There will be mixed views about whether e cigarettes should be legalised or banned. Perhaps surprisingly ASH, the pressure group where the mnemonic stands for action on smoking and health, would to a limited extent welcome these new products, they are much healthier than cigarettes or pipes or other conventional products.

There are also disputes about prostitution and whether prostitutes or the buyers of prostitution, who should face prosecution

Josephine Butler had to campaign very hard to get the age of consent for sex to be raised to 16. Prior to this child prostitution was often common. This was often due to other members of the family or sometimes employers who assumed that this was their right.

Currently, we can find as well, many debates about pornography. Whilst children are not supposed to watch films which are pornographic it is very likely that they will.

Smoking was objected to by James I in England in the early 17th century, but around 2007, smoking was prohibited in public places so that we have crimes which previously would have just been thought of as the norm.

Some forms of deviance such as laughing at a funeral would be regarded as extremely poor taste, but would have been regarded as crimes, in the 19th century by the poor, whereas now it would not be an offence.

Robert Peel, the Conservative Party Prime Minister and reformer, abolished executions from a wide variety of crime, most of which would not be considered very serious currently.

Pickpocketing was common and we can see this in some of Dickens novels, which were based on fact that even at public executions pickpocketing still took place.

Crimes for debt and debtors' prisons were common and Charles Dickens, father had been imprisoned for this. Attitudes towards debt and lending are still somewhat mixed.

According to the functionalists, deviance helps to clarify rules; it unites groups and promotes social change.

Self-examination questions

> Q1. Why might perceptions of risk be important as well as accurate views of risk? (Hint: Why might the perception of crime be important to many people?)
>
> Q2. How far can sociologists help us to determine the causes of crime and also the likely remedies of some crimes? In what ways, if at all, can different statistical methods help them?
>
> Q3. What are the problems of trying to estimate the number of crimes in the United Kingdom?

Q4. What are the limitations of data when looking at fears of crime?

Q5. What do some sociologists consider to be the relationship between ethnicity and crime/violence in society? Why might it be sensible to be cautious about drawing conclusions? Hint which groups are most likely to be stopped and searched?

Q6. How can we test whether class, income, ethnic group, gender, type of education and religious affiliations are related to crime figures?

Q7. How can we test the effectiveness of the deterrent principle?

Q8. How can prisoners and people who have been convicted of crimes be rehabilitated into society?

Q9. Which crimes cause the most problems; murders, dangerous driving, domestic abuse or large scale fraud? How can we measure these problems and what can the justice system do about them?

Q10. Should racial crimes be treated differently from other crimes?

Q11. 'Reclaim the night' was a slogan used by Feminists. What does this say about perceptions of crime?

Q12. In 2016, there were concerns that crimes involving prominent people such as the late Jimmy Saville had been covered up as part of an establishment plot. What might this suggest about the accuracy of some crime figures?

Q13. In 2016 there were apologies by the police that they had pursued too many prominent people without any serious evidence. What does this suggest about police attitudes?

Chapter 16   Climate Change, the environment and Global Warming

Awareness of the environment

People have become more aware of the environment in the UK since the 1970s and 1980s, partly because of pressure groups like Friends of the Earth and Greenpeace. It is possibly an income elastic concept i.e. that as people become richer and have more goods and services they also want to live in an area freer from pollution.

However, evidence from the government committee on climate change suggests that poorer people suffer disproportionately from climate change.

Some people have suggested that there is a trade-off between jobs and green pressures, but other people such as the founders of the Body Shop realised that they could make and sell products that were more environmentally friendly. Now there are some dedicated green shops whilst other firms will claim that their products are environmentally friendly.

Climate change

One possibility of avoiding climate change is to invest in nuclear energy but this is much more expensive than investing in renewables. Lord Deben, a former Conservative Cabinet minister made the point at a climate change meeting in 2014 that renewables are always coming down in price, whereas this is not true of most of the alternatives.

The Guardian in an article by Damian Carrington Saturday, March 19th 2016 stated that Hinkley Point C in Somerset would not possibly be able to open until 2033. The price guaranteed by the UK government commits the public to pay a subsidy to about £40 billion in real terms and provides state guarantees about both nuclear waste disposal and insurance. The price per unit of electricity generated would be three times higher than the current price, in real terms.[31]

Prof Catherine Mitchell from the University of Exeter stated that this would reduce the risk to EDF to zero, but would not help the consumer.

A spokesman for the Department of energy and climate change, however, suggested that it would bring in billions of pounds of investment into the UK and create 25,000 jobs during construction.

Why is Global Warming taking place?

Most scientists, apart from those paid by the coal or oil lobbies, accept that global warming is taking place. One of the reasons for this is that if we deplete the ozone layer, this will mean that temperatures become more extreme. It is rather similar to having a blanket on oneself that will prevent us getting too cold or too hot. The richest countries in the world in 2015 stated that there was a need to reduce greenhouse emissions from the richest countries. In April 2016, nearly 200 countries at a meeting in Paris signed up for the need to reduce carbon emissions.

What is the evidence for Global Warming?

Some of the evidence for global warming can be found in the loss of ice in the Arctic, which means that animals such as polar bears are very subject to risk and there have been some interesting programs on television showing the extent to which this happens. There has also been in tropical countries loss of ice on Mount Kilimanjaro, which is Africa's highest mountain in Tanzania.

What problems has it caused so far?

In the United States, hurricane Katrina (2005) created large numbers of refugees, whilst in Haiti (2010) large numbers of refugees were created with the problems caused by extreme weather conditions. In the USA, extreme weather conditions caused problems in New York which were highlighted in the film "This Changes Everything" by Naomi Klein.[32]

What would happen if we had no greenhouse gases?

If we did not have greenhouse gases, average temperatures on earth would be much lower and the surface of the earth would be like the frozen plains of Mars.

Sea levels

Global Warming will cause sea levels to rise, which will have a major impact on low-lying countries; whether this is the Netherlands, where a large amount of the land would be under threat without extensive sea defences, or countries such as Bangladesh where a large amount of the land is also vulnerable. Melting ice causes problems of rising sea levels.

What can we do about it?

As individuals, we can do something about this; which is to reduce the amount of fuel that we use. This can be done through better insulation of houses and other buildings, since domestic pollution is a major part of the problem.

Currently in China the pollution from vehicles means that it is unsafe for vulnerable people to be outside, particularly in cities such as Beijing.

Governments can also do a considerable amount and the Chinese government has spent considerable amounts of money on developing solar panels which have been used in that country and exported to other countries as well. Vehicle pollution in India and the USA is also extremely high.

Similarly heat extractors which use the latent heat from the air and are therefore very fuel efficient and cheap to run have been developed considerably in China.

There are alternative sources of fuel as well, including solar energy, and Kenya at the present time is aiming to be one of the leaders in using solar energy. It seems somewhat surprising, that a rich country such as Australia which is experiencing extremely bad weather, (i.e. very high temperatures which had contributed to vast numbers of forest fires) has taken less interest in the use of solar power when it is an obvious natural resource.

Using electricity more for railways

There is considerable scope in the UK for more electrification. For example, the railway line from Paddington to Cardiff and Swansea is being electrified. Crossrail's Elizabeth line extends from Reading in Berkshire through London to Shenfield in Essex, and will help passengers to cross London easily.

Not wasting food

Simple things such as being prepared to have less packaging and also to have slightly different shaped vegetables and fruit would help. In the United Kingdom, it has been estimated by Christian Aid that about 1/3 of all food which goes into the supermarket trolleys is wasted and this is this does not account for the large quantities of fruit and vegetables that are not sold to the supermarkets as they are the wrong size or shape.

Using electric or hybrid cars

It would be possible to use electric or hybrid cars which would reduce emissions in the first place.

One of the obstacles to using such vehicles is the limited number of places where refuelling can take place compared with the large number of garages where motorists, motorcyclists and lorry drivers can obtain diesel or petrol. Japan in 2016 announced that it now has more garages where batteries can be recharged than conventional garages.

Electric vehicles have the advantage of a longer life generally than diesel or petrol vehicles. If people lease their cars rather than buy them outright, in 2016, the cost is reasonably comparable.

Volvo announced in 2016 that by 2025 it aims to sell more than 1 million electric vehicles per year to UK buyers. It announced that it would launch its first full electric cars in 2019. It also announced that it wishes to be carbon neutral overall by 2025 as its contribution towards combating climate change.

Climate change and the effect on the poor

Global warming is recognised by many people, including scientists and businessmen, as a chief concern for the 21st century. Christian Aid says that this will particularly affect the poor in large numbers. The Intergovernmental Panel on Climate Change (IPCC) has warned about the effect of global warming. It will also affect government expenditure such as more flood defences in the UK. Sociologists have not always taken very much interest in the problem.

Need to look at global warming

Looking at fuel use generally we will see that this is a major problem whether for the domestic or the industrial sector and that as North Sea oil reserves diminish or at least become more difficult to obtain, then we should be looking at this. Many environmentalists would suggest that global warming is the major issue though this was hardly an issue mentioned in the 2015 U.K. general election.

Irrational concerns about wind turbines

In the 21st century rejecting wind turbines because they spoil the view of some householders may be rational if people solely look at their house prices but is irrational if global warming takes place so that many areas become uninhabitable. The alternative might be to have very expensive flood defences.

Mars Corporation and wind turbines

Mars, which is a well-known confectioner, although it produces many other products, has developed a large collection of wind turbines in the USA.

The following is the press statement from them:

By partnering with Sumitomo Corporation of Americas and BNB on a new 118 turbine wind farm, it marks the biggest long-term commitment to renewable energy use of any food manufacturing business in the United States McLean, VA – Mars, Incorporated, in partnership with Sumitomo Corporation of Americas, announced an agreement today on a new 200MW wind farm that will generate 100% of the electricity needs of Mars' U.S. operations, which is comprised of 70 sites, including 37 factories and 25,000 Associates. 'Mesquite Creek Wind,' a 118turbine wind farm was jointly developed by Sumitomo and BNB Renewable Energy and is based near Lames, Texas with a footprint of 25,000 acres. With an annual output of over 800,000 megawatthours, the energy created from the wind farm will represent 24% of Mars' total global factory and office carbon footprint – equivalent to the electricity required to power 61,000 U.S. households. The wind farm represents the biggest long-term commitment to renewable energy use of any food manufacturing business in the United States. The wind farm is one of the ways Mars is achieving its goal to make its operations 'Sustainable in a Generation' by eliminating greenhouse gas emissions by 2040. In the shorter term, has committed to 03/12/2015 Mars Moves Towards Carbon Neutral Operations With Massive Wind Farm That Will Provide Electricity From Renewable Sources Equal To Its ... http://www.mars.com/global/ presscenter/presslist/newsreleases.aspx?SiteId=94&Id=5629 2/3 reduce fossil fuel energy and greenhouse gas emissions by 25% by 2015, using 2007 as its baseline year. The Mesquite Creek wind farm will enable Mars to meet this 2015 goal. BNB, the originating developer of the wind farm, began discussions with Mars and brought Sumitomo Corporation in to the joint venture. Sumitomo Corporation and Mars, Incorporated have reached contractual arrangements that allow Mars to receive all the renewable energy certificates from Mesquite Creek, offsetting the energy use for Mars' entire US facilities. Barry Parkin, chief sustainability officer at Mars, Incorporated, commented, "We are committed to doing our part to limit climate change. We are therefore delighted to be announcing this major renewable project that takes us a big step towards our goal of becoming carbon neutral in our operations. This is an innovative approach that makes great business and environmental sense." "We are pleased to be partnered with Mars to help them reduce their carbon footprint and allow their electricity to be carbon neutral in the U.S. Mesquite Creek is a landmark project for Sumitomo and our sixth renewable energy investment in the U.S., further strengthening our commitment as a major developer and owner of renewable energy," said William Cannon, Vice President, Sumitomo Corporation of Americas. "By making this extraordinary commitment to buy renewable energy, Mars is sending a clear message that companies, private and public, have the power to lead the world on climate change. It's good for the bottom line, it's good for the environment, and projects like this leave a lasting legacy of values we hold dear. Thank you Mars and Sumitomo," said Jonathan Butcher, Sr., a founder of BNB. Development of Mesquite Creek began in 2008 on the 25,000 acre site, which is located in Borden and Dawson Counties, Texas, about eight miles from Lames. Blattner Energy Inc. is constructing the wind farm, and electricity will be generated via 118 1.7MW GE turbines. Turbine delivery is scheduled to begin at the end of the summer, with commercial operations expected to commence in the second quarter of 2015. To learn more, visit http://www.mars.com/carbonneutralby2040.

Solar energy

Sometimes simple things such as solar lights would help people particularly in poorer countries where there is no mains electricity, to be able to work in the dark.

Solar radios have the advantage, particularly in poorer areas, of enabling people to be able to receive education. Solar calculators are very useful, particularly in areas where there is no mains electricity.

Even apart from this, they have the advantage of a long-life and not needing comparatively expensive batteries.

What can schools do about climate change?

Sharing cars to and from work or school would also help. In the United Kingdom, some schools have a "walking bus" where children go in groups to school with a leader at the back and front, which both helps to enable students to socialise as well as to become fitter. Having more facilities for bikes would also help.

Vehicle pollution and number of deaths

Even apart from the effects on climate change, pollution kills many people, for example, a cross-party report on road vehicle pollution, published in 2010 chaired by the then Conservative MP Tim Yeo stated that around 30,000 people per year died from this.

Electricity companies devoted to renewables

Some electricity companies such as Good Energy and Ecotricity aim to only use renewables for generating electricity. For more details about Good Energy the book principles of business and management by David Spurling, John Spurling, James Gachihi and Simon Cruikshank can help.

Encouraging cycling

It has often been assumed that cycling is an example of an inferior good i.e. that as incomes rise people will turn to other modes of transport and so if a country had higher incomes it would have less cycling. The assumption was that in a developed country we would expect to find that demand for car transport would be regarded as a normal good or service whilst cycling might well be regarded as an inferior good or service. However, this is not necessarily be true in all developed countries since for example in the Netherlands, Denmark and Germany, cycling is regarded as an ordinary activity and in these countries many commuters travel by bike. Indeed, in Germany, although car ownership is much higher than in the UK, the bike share of trips in Germany is almost ten times higher than in the UK according to Pucher and Buehler. The government had hoped that following British success in cycling events in the Olympics 2012 and in Brazil in 2016 that more people would take up cycling in the UK. In the London area, it has become easier to hire bicycles at many railway and underground stations for a relatively small charge.

Data about cycling

One of the criticisms of data in the UK that until relatively recently data for walking or cycling was often virtually non-existent. The National Travel Survey in 1976 to 1977 provided more data.

In China, cycling has been a conventional form of transport for many people and with pollution levels very high in many cities, concern has been expressed about the increase which will occur if unconstrained car use in line with the great economic growth continues.

Government encouragement for cycling

Currently the government has said that it wants to encourage cycling partly for environmental reasons and partly because cycling is a healthy activity. However, the whole amount spent on the Sustrans national network is only £200 million and even the funding available for the existing six demonstration towns as well as new cycling towns is less than £100m. These figures are very small compared for example with even a modest road improvement scheme. Sustrans stands for (Sustainable Transport) and the cycle network extends from Inverness in North Scotland to Dover in Kent. Following a poll by the Peoples national lottery, an extra £50m has been made available to Sustrans, where it was the winner from 4 applicants. However, this does seem an odd way of funding transport projects.

Evaluation of Accident Rates and cycling

There are a number of ways of looking at accident rates. One of the commonest but not necessarily the best is to look at the number of injuries or deaths per billion passenger kilometres travelled. On this basis air transport is undoubtedly the safest with less than 0.1 per billion passenger kilometres and motor cycling is the worst. Motor cycling accident rates are about 38 times higher for than for cars used in 2005 (source of information section 7 Transport Trends). This analysis of accident rates may be sensible if we are looking at the best method to travel from A to B by different modes of transport. We are not necessarily comparing like with like, since many journeys that are now undertaken by air would probably not have been taken by other modes of public transport. This would include many holidays from the UK to the Caribbean and even more to Australasia. If, however we assume that there are time constraints to the amount of time which people want to spend travelling to and from holidays, we could try to evaluate risk by the likely accident rate per unit of time e.g. one hours travelling. If as some people suggest we get space travel as one form of holiday, then this will become even more important. One accident per 1 billion km of space travel would be a high risk per hour, whereas if cycling it would be a very low risk.

There is also the point that some modes of transport will improve health so that it is probable that if people are put off cycling because of fears of safety the improvements of health through cycling may more than offset the risk to health of accidents. The choice of words may be important. In an otherwise excellent report in the Green Paper on transport in 1977, it was stated that cycling was dangerous. This is untrue. What is dangerous is mixing cycling with other forms of transport.

A criticism of the land use planning system

A criticism of the planning system was that most of the planners had a highway engineering bias and therefore insufficient attention was paid to using other modes of transport. Perhaps because most of the decisions are made by middle aged car owners too little attention seems to have been given to walking or cycling though both modes can be important.

Since the rich usually make the decisions about transport, facilities for pedestrians and cyclists are often neglected in favour of more prestigious methods of transport. Cycling has the advantage that it only needs a minimal width compared with conventional roads.

Cycles as freight vehicles

Whilst cycles are usually thought of as a passenger vehicle the North Vietnamese showed in the civil war in the early 1970s that loads of up to 300 lbs (140 kg) could be carried. The use of separate cycle ways would open up more employment opportunities to the poor since they would then be able to take longer distances to and from work. At the present time, poor standards of road maintenance as well as poor driving standards means that many cyclists are deterred. A World Bank report on urban transport implied that cycleways are an efficient use of investment.

Cycle Tracks

Cycling is non-polluting and even if battery operated cycles are used there is little pollution or noise. Cycle maintenance is cheap and can lead to self-sufficiency compared with imports of expensive cars. Additionally, much less land is used for parking space.

Because cycling and motor cycling is much more common in the newly industrialised countries even in wealthy countries such as Singapore than in most long developed countries there may be a need for bus lanes and also for separate provision of tracks or roads for cycles and motorcycles.

Cycling and the terrain

Whilst in the UK it is often claimed that cycling is only appropriate to countries like Holland which is flat, it should be remembered that the majority of Eastern England is extremely flat.

Green travel policies

Some firms have adopted a green travel policy, which tries to encourage people to use public transport, cycling or walking or if these are not possible to encourage car sharing.

Some firms notably Body Shop have tried to encourage their workers to come to work by bike, and some local authorities have adopted a scheme whereby cycles can be subsidised. The logic of this from the local authority's point of view is that car parking space is expensive to provide whereas cycle sheds are cheap. There seems to be no reason why for short distances cycling allowance should not be at the same rates as cars. In order to encourage people to cycle, cycle lockers might need to be provided.

Combining cycling with other modes of transport

Some countries notably Sweden have long distance buses, which can carry bikes so that in semi-rural areas that people can often use their bikes for relatively short distances, but leaving the bus to go along the main road for longer distances.

There has been considerable controversy about carrying bikes on trains. The rail operators have suggested that bikes take up room, but since in very few cases i.e. only in the peak is the capacity fully used the marginal cost of providing for bikes is usually negligible.

Effect of climate change on migration patterns

Many climate change experts have predicted that if we get considerable climate change for example in countries such as Bangladesh then there will be more pressure to migrate.

Access to clean water will become more difficult and this will add to the push factors for migration.

Self-examination questions

Q1. The Governor of the Bank of England has stated that climate change is a major problem for all countries at the present time. What can individuals as well as governments do about this?

Q2. In 2016 nearly 200 countries signed up to try to reduce the likelihood of global warming and climate change affecting future economic growth? Why would international cooperation be very helpful in trying to achieve this objective?

Q3. Why might younger people have more of a vested interest in climate change than older people? How could schools and colleges help to prevent climate change?

Q4. What would be the effects on society if people used hybrid or electric cars rather than petrol or diesel engines?

Q5. What obstacles are there to people using hybrid or electric cars?

Q6. What will be the effects on global warming if more electric trains are used for both passengers and freight rather than diesel trains?

Q7. Bicycles can be hired cheaply at many railway stations in the London area. What are the advantages to the railway companies of this? What are the advantages to the other stakeholders including London residents and people working in offices in London?

Q8. How might local authorities try to encourage pedestrians and cycling in their area and what obstacles if any are there to be overcome?

Q9. Developing countries need to take more account of the needs of the poor, and this would mean paying more attention to cycling and providing better pavements etc as well as concentrating on reducing the number of accidents. How far is this true?

Q10. Why might it help both business organisations and society generally if business organisations adapt green travel plans?

Q11. Why might climate change lead to more potential migration particularly from poorer countries?

---

31 [Damian Carrington, "Hinkley Point C nuclear deal contains £22bn 'poison pill' for taxpayer", The Guardian, 18 March 2016, https://gu.com/p/ht3v]
32 See also [Naomi Klein, "This Changes Everything: Capitalism vs. the Climate", Simon & Schuster, New York, 2014, ISBN: 978-1-4516-9738-4]

Chapter 17 — Globalisation

Globalisation and Power of the Large Firms

There is often much talk about the world's largest economies. However, less attention has been paid to the power of the transnational corporations. Of the world's 100 biggest economies, the balance is almost equally divided between countries and corporations. Organisations such as General Motors, Walmart and ExxonMobil each have larger economic outputs than the 50 least developed economies.

These large organisations are well able to move their resources between one country and another. This, however, partly depends upon the industry. For General Motors the time taken to build a new car or to launch a new type of car would be quite considerable. On the other hand, Walmart may be able to take over an existing supermarket chain quickly. In the United Kingdom Walmart took over Asda which is one of the biggest retailers. Walmart will have much economic power but it is unlikely to want political power –in equal measure, except when trying to influence planning decisions in its favour. ExxonMobil, on the other hand, will be much more aware of different political changes since the price of tax of petrol is largely determined by the amount of tax that governments impose. ExxonMobil is the name of the company but in the United Kingdom is better known as Esso. It is therefore more likely to want to lobby governments, or in the U.S.A, to get it to allow new prospecting in places such as Alaska which might be viewed unfavourably by different governments.

One of the features of globalisation nowadays is that information is very quickly available across all of the major countries, including the less economically important countries. This can be easily seen in the money market where every day on television we can see the differences in the exchange rates. We can also see changes in the major stock exchange prices whether in Japan, the USA or the UK.

The power of the money market was readily shown when Britain left the European monetary system (EMS) in September 1992 and interest rates in the UK rose from 10% to 15% in one day. At the time, many people, irrespective of their feeling about the desirability or undesirability of the EMS, sensed that the ability of speculators to force government to change economic polices was undesirable. What is certain is that the concept of national economic sovereignty in an era of free exchange markets is very dubious. If people can switch currencies quickly then it is difficult to see how very different interest rates can apply in different countries. This would occur when there are very strong reasons, for example, people are very concerned about the strength of that particular currency whether for economic or political reasons. OPEC countries which gained vast amounts of money as a result of the increase in oil prices in the early 1970s have often had hot money; that is, money which is looking for the highest safe rate of interest. George Soros (1930 to date) who made a name and a fortune for himself by his ability to both forecast currency fluctuation and also by being an active player in it was accountable to no one but himself. There have been suggestions that there should be a small tax on large-scale currency movements. The Tobin tax named after the economist James Tobin (1918 – 2002) is such a tax, but it is difficult to see how this could be applied. The effects of globalisation can be seen more dramatically in many third world countries where if interest rates go up for domestic reasons in the USA or the western European economies, the citizenry will have to pay large amount of money as they repay their debts to the West.

Whilst successive governments have talked about the need for research and development, most of it is defence orientated and most of the academic research done is directed towards the needs of the multinational firms. The money spent on defence is rarely scrutinised in the same way that it is when money is spent on social security and most economics books do not scrutinise the money either. Some multinationals have endowed chairs, that is, the name given to the way that a department or sometimes a professor may be appointed within a university.

The events of September 11th 2001 in America shows that there is vulnerability in our societies that needs to be addressed. If a relatively small group of people can distort an economy so easily we may have a choice between either trying to deter them almost entirely by force of arms or alternatively trying to find out what causes the radicalism in the first place. It is unlikely that the sociologist or anyone else can stop the people who are likely to be suicide bombers. On the other hand, the amounts of sympathy that such people might have might well be diminished by taking a more constructive view of what people feel aggrieved about and then acting accordingly. President Donald Trump has tapped in to the feeling of aggrievement by many people following his unexpected election victory in 2016.

Global warming is recognised by many, including scientists and businesspeople, as a chief concern for the 21st century. Christian Aid says that this will particularly affect the poor in large numbers. The Intergovernmental Panel on Climate Change (IPCC) has warned about the effect of global warming. The changing climate will also affect government expenditure such as more flood defences in the UK. Sociologists have not always taken very much interest in the problem.

Bias in present research

A great deal of research meets the needs of the capitalist system. Many modern management methods taught in business studies courses assist the larger companies rather than the smaller companies. More business courses are also geared towards helping firms to become more efficient; there is hardly any countervailing power to help consumers to be more aware of their rights, though many people feel that large firms not only exploit the workers but also neglect the needs of the consumers.

In December 2003, it was reported that Microsoft was being sued by one of its rivals over anti-competitive behaviour. The rights and wrongs are not important. What is important is that even the largest companies should be subject to rules ensuring that they do not go against consumers' interest in an illegal way. In other cases, it is usually a case for unfair competition between companies. Celtel, one of two mobile service providers in Kenya, appealed to the Communications Commission of Kenya in early 2007 over what it termed as unfair competition from Safari.com, the other mobile service provider in that country.

Successive governments in the UK have stressed the need for an enterprise culture.

In many cases, apart from occasional television programmes or probing journalists, we are much less likely to be aware of the conditions where poorer people live. We see more about producing items of luxury for the richer countries of the world, whereas the needs of the poor in the Third World get less publicity, apart from Third World charities such as Oxfam and Christian Aid.

Criticisms of Globalisation by Professor Mary C. Grey

Mary C Grey, a professor at the University of Wales who describes herself as an ecofeminist liberation theologian, shows in her book "Sacred Longings: Ecofeminist Theology and Globalisation"[33] that it is often women who have suffered as a result of globalisation. She cites the case, described by John Pilger, of a factory in Saigon (now called Ho Chi Minh City) in Vietnam. The women there worked from 9am to 7pm for the equivalent of £12 per month, and had a hygiene card which they were allowed to use no more than 3 times a day for no longer than five minutes a time. She also suggests that we have become accustomed to believing that only human beings matter and that we are indifferent to almost every other living creature in life. People often show no compassion for the way in which animals were slaughtered in the BSE scare in the early 2000s, or the ways in which animal are put in very inhumane conditions for the sake of factory farming. There has been a growth of animal rights protests, such as testing on animals for cosmetic purposes and companies do not usually do this now. There have also been protests about the transport of cattle and sheep from the UK to the continent. There are some hours' restrictions but it is unclear if they are always obeyed.

Professor Grey also suggests that learning is devoted towards skills learning rather than to learn to value things for their own inherent value. There does seem to be a paradox here. If as they do, the multinationals are responsible for the production of music DVDs, then education is thought to be good if it enables us to do this more successfully. However, appreciation of music or other arts is thought to be a luxury subject. How then are people taught about the value of the arts in the first place? Her criticism of education as being geared to the needs of capitalism is very similar to Karl Marx in the middle of the 19th century.

She also suggests that some of the World Bank projects have been unhelpful for example the construction of dams such as Sardar Sarovar Dam at Narmada. This and the Gandhi canal, which is meant to solve the problem of Rajasthan, have actually helped to produce more salinity and even malaria in an area that has not previously suffered from the disease. Rajasthan is a desert area in India. It is often claimed but difficult to prove that the World Bank tends to look at projects from the point of view of richer countries rather than from that of the poorer ones. It is also claimed that it ignores the externalities of its projects, which are important.

Oil companies have often been ruthless in their request for more oil. Many of the tensions in the current world have been exacerbated by the quest for oil. It seems very unlikely that the late Saddam Hussein (1937 – 2006) would have gained the same notoriety if his country had not had oil.

The book "Taliban: Militant Islam, Oil and Fundamentalism in Central Asia" (2000) by Ahmed Rashid, shows how the oil companies have been interested in oil, with pipes going through Afghanistan and neighbouring territories. Much of the positioning by the USA government, amongst others, has been amoral.

Free Trade

Though many people have criticised the market, often there is no free market. Many countries have often protected their own products from overseas competition. The European Union has aimed at self-sufficiency in temperate climate products. This means that some countries that produce temperate climate products have suffered, such as New Zealand and Australia. The Caribbean countries that grow sugar cane have suffered as the European Union has subsidised the use of sugar beet in the EU countries.

There often seems to be confusion of free trade and capitalism lobbying. Free trade can be optimal given a number of qualifications. There is very little economic theory to support the idea that monopoly capitalism can deliver this optimal solution. A much freer trade which does not place restrictions on the exports from poorer countries or give heavy subsidies to American or European food, would be helpful. (Subsidies are the opposite of taxes; it means that a government will give money towards the producers).

Different possibilities of the 3 stage world economies

It is doubtful whether it is possible within the confines of one social science discipline to be able to fully understand a concept such as globalisation. We need to have some idea of historical development to see how globalisation has arisen. Given that commercial organisations will have their main aims as business targets such as the level of sustainable profit and turnover, we will need to borrow at least some of the economists' tools. This could include looking at economies of scale, which we might summarise as the advantages of big versus small operations. We may also need to have some idea of psychology since managers' preferences may include prestige, status and power. How far managers and firms are risk averse or risk takers is also important when we look at the restraints of any of the major firms and organisations. Political influences such as the effect of wars and moves toward intentional co-operation will also play their part. We would also need to examine how far Governments have encouraged or discouraged larger firms through monopoly legislation, implementation and enforcement of these laws. There may be a difference here: since the 1890 Sherman anti-trust Act in the USA, there have been legal constraints on monopoly in the USA. However, monopolies have still arisen in the USA.

Sociologists may be able to assist in the analysis by evaluating the ways in which society has as a whole evolved. The sociologist may also be able to examine the differences in culture and the way in which these are changing. The cross-disciplinary approach should not surprise us. Whatever one might think of Karl Marx, he used a number of different disciplines in order to put forwards his theories about capitalism.

The early sociologists, including Karl Marx and Weber, were very interested in the division of labour. Clearly, in global firms, division of labour can be extreme. Also in many cases, components are interchangeable between different products, which make it easier to swap the locations of factories. It probably becomes even easier in modern times, where the emphasis is less on heavy industry such as steel and oil refining. Much more production is contained within relatively small industrial units that can be duplicated almost anywhere.

Many modern businesses have an American base. The best-known is probably Microsoft, formed by Bill Gates, whose products can be seen virtually all around the world. Car companies such as Ford have some monopoly power. This has changed with the credit crunch. The widespread use of the English language has made it easier for IBM to dominate the computer world and then Microsoft to dominate the software industry.

One of the best-known sociologists in this field has been Immanuel Wallerstein, born in 1930. He has developed world systems theories, which have aroused considerable interest if not necessarily overwhelming acceptance. In order to put forward a world systems theory he has had to use cross-disciplinary boundaries in his theories using parts of economics, history and politics as well as sociology. He suggests we could have a number of possibilities for example; we could have a world empire. One of the longest lasting empires was that of the Romans which existed before Julius Caesar invaded England briefly in 55 and 54 BC and continued to about 476 AD. The Romans dominated most of Western Europe but not Scotland, and Hadrian's Wall shows the limit. The Roman influence can still be seen in the Latin languages such as Spanish and Italian. Though the English use the word 'Anglo Saxon' to describe their culture about 2/3 or more of the words they use have Latin roots. It does mean that even now it will usually be easier for an English person to be able to learn a Latin language such as French or Spanish more easily than a Germanic language such as German, Dutch, and Swedish. Though Latin is often described as a dead language, it was widely used in the Roman Catholic Church services for a long while. It was therefore possible for Roman Catholics to be able to go from one country to another and still be able to follow the church services. The effect of the British Empire, one of the largest that there has ever been and now renamed the Commonwealth, can still be seen in the widespread use of the English language in the former colonies and dominions. The reason why India can obtain some service jobs, e.g. call centre workers, from the UK is that historically many of the Indian population will have English as one of their languages. We can also see it in the UK roads where Watling Street, which ran from Canterbury, Kent, to St Albans, Hertfordshire, is the main highway for much of the A2, which runs from London through Canterbury to Dover.

World empires

The American government does not have an empire in the formal sense that the British had until the 1950s and 1960s. The American economy is sufficiently dominant that a downturn in the American economy clearly has a great effect on many other economies. Even a change in one sector such as the tourism industry will have significant effects on other countries. This was shown internationally after the destruction of the World Trade Centre building on September 11th 2001. Its effects reverberated in many countries of the world through travel patterns. It was also shown in the UK when many Americans were deterred from visiting the UK because of exaggerated fears about the extent of Bovine spongiform encephalopathy (BSE), more commonly known as mad cow disease. The phrase; 'if Wall Street sneezes the rest of the world catches a cold' may be slightly exaggerated but does have some truth. This was vividly shown in the 1930s following the Wall Street crash (1929). The American stock exchange market led directly to the great depression, which affected many countries including the USA, the UK and the Commonwealth. It has also been shown with the credit crunch.

There is a strong influence in terms of the language used in films as well as in the success of the keyboards and computer software such as Microsoft Windows. A major possibility according to Malcolm Waters ("Globalisation", 1995) is that of the world economies. We could argue that the European Union, which increased to 28 countries in 2013, is in this position as there is currently free movement of people and goods and services. This will be 27 countries following Brexit. We can also see the U.S.A as a major economy in its own right irrespective of Canada and Mexico who also belong to the North American Free Trade Area (NAFTA). It is unclear what will happen to the North American Free Trade Area following Donald Trump's election.

Waters also saw semi periphery groups of countries that were largely dependent on the core countries. This would presumably include many of the poorer Eastern European countries including Turkey, which not only hopes to enter the European Union, but has also, had its citizenry living in Germany. Many of these emigrants will send back money to their native countries and Turkey, like many others, is heavily reliant on this. Other poorer Eastern European countries include Bulgaria and Romania, which entered the European Union in 2007, Croatia in 2008 and Bosnia in 2013.

In February 2004, the then Labour Prime Minister Tony Blair announced that he was setting up a commission which would look at the problems of Africa as a whole. One of the commissioners appointed would be Bob Geldof, founder of Band Aid in 1984. It could be argued, as always, that trade would have been better than aid, since better access for agricultural products by both the European Union and the USA would have had more effect.

The third group would be the periphery states. These states are very reliant on the core states. This would include many of the sub-Saharan countries, which in many cases have not had any significant increase in per capita income and generally lack economic growth and development due to such social ills as poverty and disease. The domination of the drugs market by a few companies usually from the richer countries has also had a disproportionate effect on these poorer countries where drug prices cannot be afforded.

The chemical companies would claim with some justification that in order to do expensive research, patents are necessary so that they can be recompensed for the research and development. On the other hand, because they seek generally to get the money back with an average cost pricing policy it means that the people who need drugs, which tend to be expensive on this method of pricing, will not receive the treatment. One possibility would be to have a lump sum paid by government, which would enable the drugs company to recover their costs whilst leaving the poorer countries to be able to get the drugs and then decide how it could be distributed.

World socialism

The Marxists have argued in the past in favour of world socialism. When Nikita Khrushchev 1894 -1971 (Russian leader 1955 - 1964) in the early 1960s said, "We will bury you" it was not meant, as some people thought, as a threat to wipe out other countries by military force but by the domination of the Russians through economic achievement. The Russian space mission had destroyed some of the illusions of the west (particularly the USA) that Russia was technologically a backward country. However, the collapse of the Soviet Union around the end of the 1980s and the transition of countries such as China into using capitalist methods even whilst remaining nominally communist means that currently it seems unlikely that world socialism will dominate.

It is often difficult to find out what has happened in some of the more secretive countries. At the time of the cold war we could find examples of propaganda in many different ways with some suggesting that Russia was a worker's paradise, while for others Russia had been moving backwards since the revolution in 1917.

Problems of the 3-state model

Whilst Wallerstein's model seems to have been influential it is not difficult to find examples of countries which do not seem to fit the model.

Albania, under its late dictator Enver Hoxha 1908-1985 was very isolationist and was not one of the countries which was reliant on other countries, as the three part of the periphery model would suggest. The semi periphery states reliant on other countries for their trading do not very well fit the model. Do we assume that as in 1945 or before that Japan was a poor country by almost any standards and that it has been exploited by the west? In practice, it received a large amount of aid from the USA partly to combat the effect of what the Americans would have seen as a communist threat in the 1950s. It has subsequently become one of the major economies of the world.

The countries that belonged to Comecon before the ending of the Soviet Union around 1990, were in theory economic partners of the communist union. They were in practice very much subservient to that of the Soviet Union. Countries such as Bulgaria, Poland, Hungary, East Germany and Czechoslovakia (now divided into separate countries, the Czech Republic and Slovakia) would have been part of this union. Some other communist countries such as Yugoslavia under Tito remained relatively independent, and Albania was generally more associated with China than with Russia.

The Commonwealth is very much a free association of members and members are free to leave or join, as with Mozambique (a former Portuguese colony). Sociologists can argue that the UK and other rich countries do not do enough to help. Until the 1960s, the sterling area was important with many countries having their currencies linked to the pound. This included most Commonwealth countries, except Canada, but also included the Republic of Ireland. It was partly for this reason that the British government was so reluctant to devalue the pound (Sterling) until it was forced to in 1967. The sterling area meant that because currencies were tied to a fixed exchange rate with the pound it was relatively easy to trade without the uncertainties that have existed since that time. We could also argue that post WWII Marshall Aid does not fit in with the model. Marshall Aid gave money to the countries that were defeated or devastated by the war, such as Japan and Germany.

Some people might well feel that we need a new equivalent of Marshall Aid again. In 2006, it was argued that Darfur (Western Sudan) could have had peace for the relatively small amount of £100 million. Stability is often linked to economic development. A country with low rates of unemployment is less likely to turn to force to overthrow its government if the majority of people who want to work can do so.

It can also be argued that with the possible exception of the USA, most of the western countries including the U.K, France and Germany may be rich by other countries standards, but, because of trade with other countries, they are not able to make decisions on their own without reference to what is happening in other countries. In the early 1990s, it became obvious that if the UK had very high rates of interest compared with other countries and there were no restrictions on foreign exchange, this would soon lead to a vast flow of money outwards from the country including hot money. (Hot money is money that is not required by the holders immediately so that it can be invested quickly into any resources which is likely to be profitable).

Effect of broadly similar laws

The legal framework within the Commonwealth is often very similar, and whilst all countries have their own laws, they will be reasonably comparable to the British, in terms of contract law and operations at the House of Commons (Parliament).

Experience of the original six members of the European Union

Whilst the original six countries of the European Community (France, Italy, West Germany, the Netherlands Luxembourg and Belgium) had shared the same experience of being overrun at some stage during the Second World War, this was not true of some of the later entrants. Both the Republic of Ireland and Sweden had remained neutral during the Second World War. The original impetus for the European Union then was political. The founders (particularly the politicians who had often experienced both world wars) were determined that Europe should not go through the same experience again. They thought that giving the Germans the opportunity to sell manufactured goods, the French the opportunity to have access to a large market for its agriculture and the Netherlands the opportunity to use its specialty in transport would mean that there would be sufficient commercial ties so that there would be no opportunity for war. Several of the 2004 EU new members such as Poland and Hungary and the Czech Republic have been part of the Russian sphere of influence so their people have different memories of post Second World War history to those of the original six.

Similarities between Global Organisations

The oil companies

Some of the largest organisations, companies such as Shell or BP, consider research and development are important, but their products are homogenous. Petrol is much the same although there may be slight variations, for example, between unleaded and leaded. The research and development has often led to new uses for previously unused products. It has been estimated that there are now about 2000 derivatives of oil products. The effect of this was perhaps most widely seen at the time of the OPEC price rise in the 1970s, when many ordinary people, who probably did not associate plastics with oil, soon realised that an increase in oil prices led to much wider price rises than might be expected.

The cost of setting up new oilfields is enormous and can only really be carried out by a large firm or by a government. The sudden dramatic reduction in oil prices in 2015 lead to uncertainty about whether oil production would be so profitable in the future. In 2016, Saudi Arabia's government announced that it was considering part-privatising Saudi Aramco, the state-owned petrochemical company. The announcement was significant since commentators pointed out that the company would be the biggest in the whole world having a turnover several times that of Apple.

Boeing Domination of aircraft manufacturing

Boeing has concentrated on aircraft manufacturing and has long dominated the world market.

The high costs of research and development in these fields have been offset by the economies of scale enabling them to sell to most of the world's airlines as can be seen at any major airport. Concorde the supersonic plane cost around £1 billion to develop. Ironically, the Russian communist government at that time also tried to develop a similar aeroplane. Several European governments have joined together to form a consortium to enable the airbus program to go ahead since it is beyond the reach of countries such as the UK to do it alone. Currently Boeing has produced the Dreamliner so the European Airbus will be competing with this. The larger aircraft has the advantage of economies of scale so that it gives a cheaper cost per passenger kilometre than previous aircraft.

The airlines themselves have gained from a favourable taxation regime compared with most other transport organisations and the private car. This has been increasingly obvious as the British government is trying to put forwards a long-term view for airports that assumes that the favourable taxation system for airlines will remain for the next thirty years. The problem is more difficult as one country cannot alone try to impose higher taxes on fuel or landing rights because the airlines would simply go elsewhere. If the problem is to be contained, then international coordination would help.

Computers

The major giants in the technical field are IBM (International Business Machines), Apple Mac and Microsoft. For a long while, computers and IBM seemed to be virtually synonymous. However, it made huge loses and it is currently concentrating on turning these huge losses around by focusing on mainframe computers and consultancy. For example, in 1993 it lost more than $18 billion.

Nestlé

Nestlé is in a field where research and development in the ordinary sense is unimportant, since items such as those made by Henry Isaac Rowntree (1837 – 1883), including chocolates and pastries, could be made by many small firms. It has also grown through acquisition for example through the acquisition of Shredded Wheat, which is still one of the major cereals eaten in the UK. The key here is marketing and customer knowledge. Critics have suggested that Nestlé, and most chocolate makers, have paid very low wages to the producers of cocoa, one of the essential ingredients of chocolate. Nestlé has run into strong criticism about the way it markets its baby food.

Nestlé has become a major food corporation and has taken over other businesses such as Rowntree. It also has an interest in cereal companies such as Nabisco Shredded Wheat and Carnation milk. Nestlé has been widely criticised for promoting baby milk. This is because often fresh water is not available so that whilst the baby food itself is healthy, the food given to the baby is not, so that breast milk would be much better. There have also been other developments such as the launch of café direct which on the coffee market will be probably only a minor challenge to Nestlé as it has its own giant in the field; Nescafe.

Globalisation of the media

Procter and Gamble have remained as one of the two giants in the detergent field competing with Unilever in the UK market. Here also, the key seems to be marketing since inherently there is little difficulty in making soaps. The term soap which is commonly used around the world to mean popular weekly televisions programmes, also known as telenovelas, such as Neighbours in Australia, Wingu la Moto in Kenya, Coronation Street in the UK, got their names from the kind of television advertising that soap manufacturers such as Procter and Gamble used to make. The intense advertising makes it difficult for new firms to enter the market but there has been increasing competition from the supermarkets' own brands (in the UK) since they have sufficient selling power to do this.

Giddens writes about the globalisation of the media. One of the factors in this is the growth of television and the media. During the first Gulf War, many people watched coverage from some of the American TV stations such as CNN. In many hotels, the cable TV networks show American channels. In his 1989 book,[34] Giddens writes about the importance of British programmes since many of them are exported to the USA. Since writing his book, the BBC in particular has greatly extended its sales. This includes nature programmes, which will have a wide appeal since they are not devoted to any one culture. The BBC has also sold many of its comedy programmes to many countries. It has also exported wildlife programmes especially those made by David Attenborough. However, the U.S.A is by far the biggest producer of TV programmes. In the UK and other Western countries except the USA, national newspapers have relied heavily on the Reuters organisation for their sources of information.

The use of the Internet has made it much easier for people to be able to communicate with each other. Presently, it is more widely used by middle class rather than working class people for communication.

Does global culture ignore all national boundaries?

It is sometimes argued on the other hand that a global culture will ignore all cultural difference. This does not necessarily seem to be true. McDonalds has had to adapt to make inroads into a country with a mainly Hindu tradition such as India. Hindus regard the cow as sacred, thus beef-burgers can obviously not be part of the menu.

The book, "McDonaldization of Society" (1993), by Professor George Ritzer of the University of Maryland shows how McDonalds - the fast food company - has not only become a world-wide institution, but also how its methods have become part of the global economy.

Professor Ritzer states that the main aim of McDonalds is to get food as quickly as possible. He also points out that the use of computers has helped to make everything more predictable. The main advantage of McDonalds is the consumers' belief that they get a lot of food relatively cheap. He suggests the same ideas have also applied to other institutions such as education, since even if students have a tick list on how their lecturer is doing, it can help the lecturers who do not ask too much of their students. It also means often since lecturers are judged by the number of publications it is better to produce a lot of material however badly written it is.

Culture

Though the word "culture" is widely used, its meaning, and how people identify with it, is not obvious. Whilst people on the defensive talk about British culture as being swamped by immigrants; British society like most current societies has many different cultures sometimes differentiated age groups, so that young people's preferences will often be more similar across international boundaries than with the older generations. It may also be affected by class: subsidies to the arts have often been criticised as giving the middle class the opportunity, to get cheaper tickets to the opera, to which the working class do not usually go. The male voice choirs by contrast often grew out of the shared experience of mining communities where there would have been few other facilities for entertainment. Similarly, the brass band often grew out of close-knit mining communities.

It surely depends upon different aspects of life. For instance, in music those people who like classical music could probably identify in this context with being European since many standard classical music programmes will have pieces by J. S. Bach and Beethoven -both Germans- Mozart who was Austrian and Tchaikovsky who was Russian. For literature, however we will probably find that language is more of a barrier and so many people could identity with American and British writers but fewer people will have read Johann Wolfgang Goethe 1749 -1832 who is probably Germany's best-known writer; or Ngugi wa Thiong'o of Kenya, who mainly writes in one of the country's vernaculars. For jazz the influence has been American both white and originally black.

There are increasing global influences such as TV networks like CNN and entertainment influences like Disneyland, there are still differences in other directions. Cartoons are expensive to make, but dubbing is comparatively inexpensive, so that this means that they can be shown across many countries for very little additional expense. Cable and digital television means that it is even easier to watch cartoons than where most households only had one television and no internet to catch up on the programs they have missed.

Globalisation also means that with the sports channels that many African people can watch soccer and will know the names of the Premier division clubs UK better than their own local clubs.

Whilst McDonalds can be found in many countries, the idea of a long lunch break will be more common in the Caribbean than in Europe. Similarly, the concept of a pub where the emphasis is on drinking alcohol without food will have its roots in England but is comparatively uncommon in African cultures. Some people have suggested that this is one of the explanations of binge drinking which received much publicity in the UK. Many medical staff state that there should be a minimum price for alcoholic drinks in the UK.

Differences between rural and urban cultures

There are, within a country, often major differences between what might be called the deep rural areas and the conurbations. The differences between the Western Isles of Scotland and London or Glasgow are deeper than the differences between many of the major cities such as London and Paris. The deep rural area, means areas where many people live and obtain their money from the local primary activities of farming, fishing, and forestry or related processes like cheese or butter making. This would be in contrast to people who live in the country when they just sleep in the countryside but obtain their living, do their shopping and get their entertainment from the conurbations or large towns. Some of the Scottish Western Isles will have a very strong view about Sunday as a holy day and thus have sternly opposed flights to and from the Isles on Sundays. They will also often have a much more puritan view of life than will be found in a cosmopolitan city such as London.

Differences in patterns of shopping

Although supermarkets dominate in most countries they offer low prices partly because they pay less money to their employees. However, in many of the continental countries of Europe, the patterns of shopping seem quite different. People in Austria will more often use the local farmer's market. They will use old-fashioned baskets to go shopping and to get bread daily.

Supermarkets exist but have not dominated to such an extent as in the Anglo-Saxon cultures. In many European countries people, will travel greater distances to get to the local markets, particularly on Saturday where the emphasis is often on fresh good food rather than on the cheapest. This can also be seen in African countries, where they even have 2 or 3 market days in a week. Online shopping is altering shopping habits in many countries.

Economists have often stressed the concept of comparative advantage, but it is difficult to see how this applies to much of modern trade, where one has almost identical products, for example, 1100 cc cars in most Western countries. The concept of product differentiation, which is linked to marketing, seems a more plausible explanation of what is happening at the present time. We could argue, therefore, that much of what is happening is due to effective marketing rather than being due to comparative advantage in the sense that 18th century economists such as Ricardo had argued.

Global middle class and the missing working class

Whilst in the past there have been slogans such as 'workers of the world unite' it is often easier for the middle class to unite than the working class. Many of the professions and their professional bodies such as the Chartered Institute of Logistics and Transport cover many professions mainly in Commonwealth countries. The link here is that transport is often an international business and therefore there are points of similarity even for people working in domestic transport systems. Other professional bodies such as those in the accountancy field will also straddle several or in some cases many countries. In many cases, consultants and managers in a given profession will be able to move fairly easily from one job to another irrespective of the country so long as there is no major language barrier. The growth of the multinational companies makes this even more likely.

Though not much progress has been made by the European Union on the harmonisation of professional qualifications; professionals will often have the same jargon to tie them together. Common interests usually mean that international barriers are often easily broken. Many articles will be written about development in other countries as well as different emphasis on priorities of those countries. Advertisements in professional journals or on the web mean that it is relatively easy to obtain information about jobs in other countries for professional people. They may well have studied together since in some cases – particularly for older workers – there may have been relatively few colleges, which catered for some of the professional bodies.

The harmonisation of regulation on many products within the EU means that it is much easier to comply and to be aware of the legal constraints than it may have been in the past. For dangerous goods travelling by ship, the provisions have been laid down by the International Maritime Organisation so that they will be the same whatever country one is working in. This is obviously desirable since labelling of dangerous goods should obviously be instantly recognisable whether or not dock workers can read well or in only one language. Bearing in mind that the captain of the ship may be from one nationality and the crew from many others, there were strong arguments to have the same regulations. This is why Russian and American experts amongst others, managed to agree on such measures even in the middle of the cold war.

Other organisations such as the International Air Transport Association (IATA) and the UIC (Union Internationale Chemin de Fer,) have also had similar regulations. The fact that IATA exists has made it easier for travel, since one airline ticket is usually easily recognisable to all.

Unskilled workers migration

Unskilled workers can often find it easy to obtain jobs if they go from the very poorest countries to the richer ones since the local population will often not wish to carry out the menial tasks. This occurs in Western countries and some countries of the East such as Saudi Arabia and Dubai. In 2016 there has been considerable publicity about poor workers' conditions in Qatar which had been awarded the World Cup tournament for 2022. There is however unlikely to be the same community of interest except where they form a large homogenous part of the population. For the working class, there are more likely to be problems of finding suitable accommodation than for the middle class.

Sometimes there may be illegal immigrants so that the menial jobs such as those in cleaning and in the building trades and fruit picking are paid cash in hand so as to evade tax and eventual detection. The case of the Chinese cockle gatherers in Morecambe Bay who died in February 2004 drew attention to both inadequate safety procedures and to the fact that people were receiving very low wages for a dangerous occupation. Ironically, because some of them had mobile phones, the tragedy received wide scale coverage more quickly than with many other accidents in different parts of the world.

The ageing population in the UK means that we need to work longer, have more workers or radically alter our work patterns.

Types of Transnational Corporations

Many Transnational Corporations are conglomerates. Unilever makes Walls ice cream, detergents such as Surf and Persil, spread such as Stork Margarine and Blueband, and meat until it was sold off. Conglomerates cover different types of products and services. Transnationals can be sub-divided into those which Amos Perlmutter ("Modern Authoritarianism: A Comparative Institutional Analysis", 1981) calls ethnocentric ones where the head office is dominant and there is similarity in all its branches wherever they may be. On the other hand, what he calls polycentric whereby the individual firm's decisions are mainly made in the country by the local management with the role of the central organisation being to make major policy decisions. More recently however the large firms have often tried to move decision making to the centre, in order to take up the advantage of lower wage costs in other countries. The Japanese companies often managed to export their management styles, thus altering many previously dominant management styles.

Anthony Giddens also draws attention to 'agribusiness,' which means that food production has been altered with large-scale firms processing the foods. This is nothing new, Levers originally had palm oil supplies for their soap and in turn Lever Brothers became a very large food business.

Sharon Beder from the University of Wollongong in Australia shows how the large-scale companies can in many cases manipulate public opinion. She shows how from the 1970's onwards, the media machine in the USA has become gradually more important. She also points out the meanings of the various think tanks, which then become part of the main sources of news. She suggests that the Heritage Foundation in the USA is frequently used as a method of getting information across. This has been particularly important for example in the attacks on the concept of global warming and also on the effects of dioxin. Part of the problem is that the public in many cases has little knowledge of science.

Beder also draws attention to the fact that 98% of U.S.A cities have daily papers with no competition. Also, about six major corporations own most of the TV channels. She points out the great influence of GEC (General Electric Company – now defunct) which amongst other things is a major plastic manufacturer as well as a manufacturer of jet engines. She says that this can be used to give biased accounts of General Electric's actions.

Susceptibility to changes in expectations

The tourist market is very susceptible to changes in the mood of American consumers. At the time of the Gulf War in 1990 - 1991, many Americans feared travelling abroad and this had an impact on tourism, in many countries of the world. Terrorist bombs in Paris and Brussels killed relatively few people in 2015 but led to major alarms not just in France and Belgium but also elsewhere. Sociologists often talk about the importance of objective rather than subjective data. Subjective data is what people act upon, thus, it may be more important than objective data. This particularly applies to the idea of risk involved in travelling to different countries.

Differing national attitudes

Professor Grey states that the provisions of cash crops have often meant greater demand for water than crops grown in a subsistence economy where people produce mainly for themselves and sell any surplus in local markets. Friends of the Earth have also commented unfavourably on global markets, which mean that foods are grown and transported over great distances quite often at the expense of local producers. Selling in the overseas market would be subject to the problems of the cobweb theorem if the market were one of perfect competition. This means that prices can fluctuate violently. This was what Durkheim thought was wrong with modern industrial society. Often there are often monopsonies (literally a single buyer in the market) and in other cases there are oligopsonies (few buyers in the market who can force the price to become lower than if the market was a competitive one). Due to international barriers to trade by the richer countries it is more difficult to export food products for the third world countries. This would be true of cocoa products in West Africa or coffee growers in East Africa. In both cases, the price of chocolate and coffee is high while the price of the cocoa and coffee bean is a very small part of it. For this reason, the Co-operative movement in the UK has announced that in future, all its own brand chocolate will be from fairly traded resources.

Also because of subsidies paid to farmers in the west particularly in America, farmers in other countries often receive a very low wage; this would be true of sugar cane which has an almost perfect substitute with heavily subsidised sugar beet.

Genetically Modified (GM) crops

One of the main scientific issues that has aroused controversy has been that of Genetically Modified (GM) crops. Supporters of the system of GM crops have suggested that we need them to help the world's larger numbers of poor to have food. We usually have food surpluses and the EU has set aside policies, that is, paying subsidies to farmers not to grow foods. The poor of the world do not have to suffer from food shortages, they just need resources to be able to afford them. Critics on the other hand suggest that particularly if there is a terminator seed, that is, seeds that will not be self-perpetuating but will come to an end of their life that this will give even more power to that of the mass producers. They also argue that there will be cross-pollination so that people who for example would want to take part in the small but rapidly growing organic market will find that they cannot do so because their crops are contaminated. It has been difficult to find areas in the UK that are willing to go ahead with trials of GM crops. Critics have also suggested that far from the government remaining in a relatively neutral position on the issue and weighing up the costs and benefits has been very biased. Opinion polls in the United Kingdom suggest that the public as a whole seems to be against the concept of GM crops, whilst in the United States of America there is far less discussion. The UK generally has a more sceptical culture compared to the optimism in the USA.

Globalisation is important and this was a key part of the. Donald Trump's victory in the USA presidential election 2016.

Sociologists have set out to explain the workings of modern society and also to identify how it should operate in the future. Society changed in Western Europe in the 18th century with the industrial and agricultural revolutions. Among the characteristics that distinguish modern from traditional societies are that the nation state is the key political unit. The state has a territory quite often with the same cultures and sometimes with a shared language, although countries such as Canada, Belgium and Switzerland do not have a common language. Social life is organised rationally and gives a source of identity. In the capitalist system, private ownership of the means of production is in the hands of shareholders. Industrialisation meant that wealth distribution was very unequal and in 2016, press reports suggested that distribution of income was much more unequal in the UK than it had been. Class conflicts have been shown in several European countries, sometimes culminating in riots. The credit crunch 2008 onwards affected most European countries that has affected some such as Portugal and the Eastern European countries in the European Union much more. Production has been organised on what is called the Fordist principle i.e. work has become more specialist.

Early sociologists expected that scientific, secular and rational methods of thinking would dominate an industrial society. Science has become increasingly important in medicine with great emphasis on the development of new drugs to combat diseases. In 2016, the then Prime Minister David Cameron stressed the importance of concerns that antibiotics may no longer be effective. Medicines and healthcare have meant increasing lifespans. Currently there is pressure to introduce more medical tests and medicines to combat senile dementia. Sociologists, economists and politicians were all concerned about the proposed merger between Pfizer and an Anglo Swedish company AstraZeneca in 2014. The communication process has become much more dependent on the computer especially since the web was invented in 1989.

Tradition has become less important as has ascribed status. Individualism has been encouraged by the neo-liberals but how far freedom is compatible with the powers given to government to be able to snoop on emails and phone calls has become more a matter of debate since the Snowden revelations on the extent of snooping by the USA and the UK. In 2016 there was fierce debate between the government which wanted to introduce legislation quickly so that security services including MI5 would be able to survey records of emails and telephone calls whilst critics called this a snoopers' Charter. Chancellor Merkel of Germany has strongly indicated her displeasure with American snooping on her government's ministers.

Inequality has become much wider in some capitalist cultures such as the USA, UK and Australia than others such as the Nordic countries. Inequalities however are also very great in China and North Korea which are communist countries.

Technological changes

Globalisation has been caused by a number of changes. One of these is technology so that people can travel within 24 hours to almost any part of the globe. Information exchange has become very fast so that a change in conditions in a country whether the Tsunami in 2004 where the tidal wave killed many thousands of people in Asia or problems in Ukraine in 2016, are transmitted instantly. Even very oppressive regimes have not managed to stop the use of YouTube etc showing instantly what is happening. Goods can be sent very quickly so that Kenyan roses can be sold in the UK. Globalisation can also mean higher levels of pollution so that governments are more aware of global warming although short term considerations may mean that people deny this.

---

33 [Grey, Mary C (2004). Sacred Longings: The Ecological Spirit and Global Culture (1st SCM Press ed.). London; Minneapolis, MN: SCM Press; Fortress Press. ISBN: 978-0-8006-3647-0]

34 Anthony Giddens, *Sociology* (London: Macmillan, 1989) ISBN 978-0-333-42739-2

Chapter 18　　　　　　　　　Typical exam questions

This relates to Chapter 13 crime and deviance

Explain what is meant by corporate crime

Sociologists and others use the phrase corporate crime to men crimes which are committed by governments, business organisations etc. rather than by individuals.

In 2016, there are many examples of government crimes such as widespread massacres by government forces and opposition in Syria and other countries.

There are also many examples of business committing crimes such as widespread fraud by a number of different financial institutions.

Most people who have computers will find that people have tried to hack in to find details of their bank accounts or other personal details.

The banks and other financial institutions themselves have been guilty of mis-selling many products and services.

Some sociologists would suggest that there is a deviant subculture where the teenagers and also subsequently some adults will belong to this subculture and share their values rather than the norms of society which the functionalist approach suggests.

In the deviant subculture, sociologists such as Cohen: suggest that working-class boys improved their status through a deviant behaviour which they would not have gained if they had done well at school.

Explain what is meant by corporate crime

Sociologists and others use the phrase corporate crime to mean crimes which are committed by governments, business organisations etc. rather than by individuals.

In 2016 we can find many examples of government crimes such as widespread massacres by government forces and opposition in countries such as Syria.

We can also find examples of business committing crimes such as widespread fraud by a number of different financial institutions.

Most people who have computers will find that people have tried to hack in to find details of their bank accounts or other personal details.

The banks and other financial institutions themselves have been guilty of mis-selling many products and services.

Some sociologists would suggest that there is a deviant subculture where the teenagers and also subsequently some adults will belong to this subculture and share their values rather than the norms of society which the functionalist approach suggests.

We can also see anecdotal evidence about this. For example, if television crew are apparent, where there have been examples of gang violence, some of the group will be willing to play up to this image. The same will apply to people being interviewed on the radio.

Some Marxists, however, will suggest that labelling theory results in working class boys in particular being labelled as criminals because the people who deal with them whether magistrates or judges, probation officers, police officers or people from the schools whether teaching staff or administrative staff will label students as failures, whereas teenage boys who behave in the same way will not be labelled in the same way.

Apart from the concept of class we can see that the same groups in schools and people concerned with maintaining the law will often react in different ways to people from different cultures.

The enquiry into the death of Stephen Lawrence a black teenager who was killed at a bus stop in south east London showed that the police had not taken his murder seriously. This led to the police being called institutionally racist in the metropolitan area.

His mother now Lady Lawrence campaigned very vigorously to ensure that the case was taken up much more seriously.

One of the problems in testing hypotheses about crime is that there are differences between the official statistics which are recorded by the police and surveys by a variety of bodies, which give totally different figures. More details about this can be found on government websites.

One example of a longitudinal study is that from the offending, crime and Justice Survey which looked at drug use, as well as antisocial behaviour in 2004.

Some crimes such as sexual abuse, particularly by prominent figures have not been recorded accurately as the enquiry into the Jimmy Savile case showed.

Jimmy Savile had been well known person at the BBC who had presented programmes such as Top of the Pops for many years. Because of his status, he was often allowed access to places including prisons, schools etc. where even though there had been allegations about his behaviour that they were not taken seriously.

Dame Janet Smith's Report published in February 2016 highlighted the ways that he was able to manipulate the BBC and other authorities, using his status to cover-up his predatory behaviour.

Sexual abuses have also occurred within the church framework, perhaps because ministers of religion have still been regarded as honest, in spite of the decline in church membership and church attendance. Pope Francis has suggested that he wishes to identify and apologise for people who have been hurt as a result of the church being more interested in its reputation than in being interested in the victims.

Studying society

A-level examination entries by gender in Utopia 2016

Subject	Ratio of boys to girls
Computing	12 to 1
Music	1 to 5
Sociology	1 to 3

In 2016, the government is interested in why girls do not take up A-level maths and physics which are essential to engineering.

There are vacancies on engineering apprenticeships which the government would like to see filled. The government is interested because older engineers are retiring and are not being replaced.

Similarly, many doctors wish to retire in the next five years and maths and a science subject are usually regarded as essential before students can start their seven-year training before they can become junior doctors.

The costs of training doctors are very high and whilst one solution would be to recruit doctors from overseas this is not regarded as an ethical solution.

Self-examination questions

Q1. Explain one way in which sociologists might be able to help the government to understand why schools and colleges could encourage more girls to study maths and physics.

Q2. Why might it be helpful for the government to encourage careers advisors to interview a random selection of girls and boys of the relevant age group to see what factors determine their A-level studies?

Q3. Does the table above help to confirm or reject the idea of gender stereotyping? Why might this be important for a range of jobs apart from those mentioned in the above passages?

Q4. Why might it be helpful to look at study patterns in both mixed and single gender schools to see if similar patterns emerge particularly in maths and physics? What problems of bias might arise with naive data?

Q5. Why might parental aspirations be important when looking at the number of students applying to go on to higher education? Why might parental aspirations be different between different ethnic groups?

Q6. Why might sociologists be able to advise the government on how to minimise friction between different groups such as those within the NHS. Why might this be important?

Families

Q1. Explain what has happened to the divorce rate in the last 50 years in England and Wales? Why might both the UK government and local government be very interested in this?

Q2. How do changing family patterns affect the demand for housing and why is this important?

Q3. Why might extended families have a different pattern of behaviour to others in society?

Q4. Why has the number of single people in the United Kingdom increased considerably in the post-war period?

One reason is that women no longer have to get married in order to have a reasonable standard of living. The term breadwinner indicates how for many years women would not have been expected to be the main wage or salary earner but would have earned what is sometimes called pin money.

Therefore, there is less pressure to get married for this reason.

Another is that whereas having sex outside marriage would have been regarded as sinful by a large number of people there is less of a stigma to this nowadays. Therefore, people may have sex without feeling the need to get married.

More recently the increase in house prices compared to earnings has meant that it is far more difficult for younger people to obtain suitable accommodation. The term boomerang generation has sometimes been used to denote people who go to university and then returned to the family home.

The cost of a wedding typically over £10,000 may well be a deterrent to couples who otherwise might wish to get married.

Families

Q1. Explain what has happened to the divorce rate in the last 50 years in England and Wales. Why might both the UK government and local government be very interested in this?

There has generally been an increase in divorces and data can be obtained from Social Trends. The government will be interested since it will affect the demand for housing since often with a split-up people may require two houses rather than one. It will also affect education since often children will spend some of their time with one parent and some with the other parent. This makes it difficult for children to be able to complete homework or study compared with a two-parent family where supervision should be easier.

Local authorities obtain money from council tax and they need to make plans based on the number of households in the locality. Often they will have to revise their estimates if there is a divorce since some people will move out of the area.

Travel patterns will also alter and Oxford University carried out a HATS technique which stands for household activity travel surveys which shows the total demand for travel during the day.

Q2. How do changing family patterns affect the demand for housing and why is this important?

In Victorian society, many extended families often with their servants lived in large houses with several generations of the same family, especially unmarried ladies in the same house.

Q3. What is meant by the term extended family? Why might extended families have a different pattern of behaviour to others in society?

The term extended families means where more than one generation are together sometimes in the same house or sometimes living in the same locality. Willmott and Young investigated the Woodfordisation process in their book **Family and Kinship** in East London in 1957 and came to the conclusion that when people moved to Woodford in Essex that they had much less contact with their relatives and had a different style of behaviour to those in the inner cities from where they had moved.

Studies have shown that in old age many people have few people they can turn to and is one of the factors which affect the prevalence of dementia. It also means that whereas extended families often wanted large houses to accommodate three generations or sometimes four that this is no longer usually true.

Apart from this in times of crisis anyway people being able to talk to others about matters of concern reduces stress levels.

At the other end of the scale it means that celebrations often become much easier to put into effect since there are more people around to both organise and attend them. This will add quite often to social cohesion.

It can also affect children's learning since grandparents may well be an important part of the children's informal learning. It can also affect formal learning since often the parents may be able to get better jobs whilst the grandparents can carry out babysitting duties.

Q4. What is meant by the term Cohabitation? Explain what is happening to cohabitation figures in the United Kingdom and why it is happening.

The term "cohabitation" means couples who live together, without having been married or in a civil partnership. The number of people who are cohabiting has increased considerably in the United Kingdom. This is partly because of secularisation. There is now much less stigma in many people's eyes about living together. The number of people who go to church has fallen considerably. In the past living in sin, the term frequently used for cohabitation, will have discouraged many people from cohabitation.

Demographic features such as the longer life span for most people will also have played a part. Whereas in Victorian society the typical lifespan for many working-class men would have been short, this is no longer the case.

Economic factors as well can be important. In the past, the term bread winner was often used for the male in the household but by 2016 women outnumbered men in the UK Labour force. The lack of financial dependence means that women no longer have to rely on a man for their income. They may fear that marriage will reduce their independence.

Contraception will also have played a part, since men and women can now engage in sex without thinking that an unwanted child will make it more imperative to marry.

Culture and identity:

Q1. How does globalisation affect the food that we eat?

If we look at British society, it is sometimes said that curry and chips show the effect of globalisation. Curry would not have been part of the typical menu in the immediate post-war period in the UK but we in 2016 that there are many Indian and Bangladeshi restaurants and takeaways serving such food. Apart from this many other non-ethnic restaurants and cafes will also serve curries as part of their menu. Sometimes globalisation has taken place as with McDonald's where sociologists can observe the same foods being sold almost everywhere. However even McDonald's has to take account of some traditions, in India many people are Hindus and would not wish to eat beef as cows are sacred animals.

However, the foods have sometimes been modified so that curries being sold in the UK will be much less strong than would be customary in the Indian subcontinent. In 2016 the restaurant and café owners of Indian subcontinent descent wanted to ensure that even if there are immigration restrictions that they can still have enough cooks and chefs to be able to cook in their tradition.

It may also affect the times that people spend on eating. The French traditionally have always liked a long lunch break whereas Anglo-Saxon societies including the British and American have not so often had this concept.

The costs of travel have also reduced considerably, in real terms i.e. after allowing for inflation. This means that far more people have travelled to other countries, and therefore will often have experienced different types of food, whether in cafes or restaurants or sometimes buying food in the supermarkets or hypermarkets.

Q2. Explain what factors affect global music.

One of these is the ease in which music can be transmitted from one society to another this arose during the Second World War when the American influence including jazz was often strong. In the modern era, it has become much easier for people to download music very quickly. The performing rights Society wants to ensure that people producing music get paid correctly that in practice there are many counterfeit DVDs and often other countries will not bother to pursue traders acting illegally.

Apart from this television programmes such as Eurovision will be heard and seen not just by people in Europe but also elsewhere.

People can also hear music on radio programs which will transcend national borders. Barriers are breaking down as for example whereas the Cuban authorities had often wanted to ban Western-style music in 2016 the Rolling Stones performed in a free concert to around 250,000 people in Havana.

Festivals such as the Glastonbury Festival in Somerset attract large numbers of people but perhaps more importantly that they will often spread the word about different styles of music as a result

Bob Dylan would have been one of the people whose music became well-known because of such festivals. In the modern era with social networking this becomes even easier.

Q3. What is meant by the term traditional culture?

Traditional culture usually refers to the era where before the Industrial Revolution people would often have carried out activities such as spinning and weaving within households. There are traditional cultures in more remote areas of the world for example when members of the Royal family visited Bhutan in 2016 they found a country very different to most Western society. The King of Bhutan which is now a democracy has wanted the country to have values where national well-being is more important than money. The idea of traditional society would mean that people would actively participate in making decisions at work and elsewhere rather than having it imposed upon them.

Music styles would also be those arising from the experience of ordinary people. The term folk dances indicate that for many people traditionally they would have had dances reflecting the type of work that they did and also their experiences. This would have included horn pipe dancing.

Minimum wage

What were the main original concerns about having a national minimum wage in the UK? How far have these concerns been justified? Has the national minimum wage been effective in reducing poverty? In what ways, will the national living wage affect the economy?

One of the concerns expressed about the minimum wage was that some workers might lose their jobs as a result of what at first sight would seem to be a fair measure. How far this is true depends upon the types of jobs that people do. There would seem to be 4 main ways that it could lead to loss of employment, the first is that businesses could go abroad for workers, the second is that that firm could have slightly higher wage workers as a substitute, the third is that they could employ 16 –17 year olds who were not on minimum wage as a substitute and the fourth is that technology or greater use of machinery etc would mean that fewer people were employed.

If we look at some of the low paid jobs, this could include many in the fast food industry whether working in cafes, restaurants or public houses.

It is unlikely that these firms would suddenly go abroad but it might be possible to find substitutes such as using more mechanical devices including dishwashers or possibly to have more of the food processing carried out in other countries where wages are lower.

Fruit picking has been a low paid occupation in counties such as Kent which have historically attracted large numbers of people during this season. There have been continuous changes with the development of dwarf trees and these have continued.

There are also allegations that migrant workers have been employed at illegal low wages with gang masters encouraging people to come into these occupations with spurious claims.

More details about some of these can be found in the book by Felicity Lawrence "What they don't tell you about the food you eat".

Carers have been another occupation in which wages are low. Standards have not always been very good and there have been prosecutions for poor standards at some nursing homes. In 2016, some care homes have expressed concerns about the introduction of the "National Living Wage", an increase to the existing "National Minimum Wage".

Migrant workers have frequently been used as a substitute for the indigenous population.

The textile industry is one where if wages are too high it would be possible for organisations to go abroad and the textile industry both before and after the introduction of the national minimum wage has had many problems competing with overseas firms. One possible action is for the textile industry to concentrate on the higher quality textiles for example using alpaca wool rather than ordinary wool.

Cleaning is another low-paid occupation, it is one where cash in hand it is often a substitute for many workers if unscrupulous firms and employees use this.

Call centres are another low-paid occupation with intense pressure on some employees to carry out a fixed number of calls.

These jobs could have gone abroad particularly to the Indian subcontinent where many potential employees will have English as one of their spoken languages and they have often been trained to learn about English culture including football clubs if that is what callers expect to be able to be able to talk about.

The idea however that all organisations would go abroad when the minimum wage was payable is obviously nonsensical. At the time of the introduction Burger King was paying £1.20 an hour to some of its employees and clearly the fast food restaurant was not going to relocate to another country.

A variation of the minimum wage has been what the current Conservative government calls a minimum living wage. In November 2014, the UK living wage rate was set at £7.85 an hour but was £9.15 per hour in the London area. At that time KPMG one of the major accountancy firms stated that around 5 million workers were being paid less than the national minimum living wage. Whilst some employers predictably suggested that they could not afford this, others such as the Nationwide Building Society announced that they would be paying this to all their workers whatever their role.

Some nursing homes in 2016 have suggested that the national minimum wage will lead to major problems for them, especially when accommodating the most vulnerable people who have had some of their bills paid by local authorities.

What factors cause global poverty?

There is a social democratic perspective. This approach favours a redistribution of income from rich to poor. We can find examples of this in the Brandt commission report in 1970s which included a wide range of politicians including the late Sir Edward Heath the Conservative Prime Minister as well as Willy Brandt a left-wing former Chancellor of Germany. They suggest that sociologists should be involved in researching different problems and therefore attempting to have policies to eradicate these.

Chapter 19 — Glossary of terms

A

Absolute poverty

This refers to people who do not have a sufficient income to be able to afford basic shelter, food and warmth.

Whilst it is commonly thought of as a phenomenon mainly of the Third World we can also find many examples of this in richer countries such as the homeless in major cities such as London.

Ageing population

This is a common phenomenon of developed countries. It is particularly true of the United Kingdom and Japan. It often means that the proportion of people over retirement age is also increasing.

Ageism

This refers to prejudice against people of a particular age group. Whilst it is often thought of as a prejudice against older people, we also find stereotypes about young people that may prevent them being able to obtain jobs.

Agencies of social control

These are the organisations attempting to control people's behaviour. This would include government at all levels as well as families, employers, schools and colleges, religious authorities and the mass media.

Agenda setting

This refers to the media and pressure groups being able to focus attention on particular issues. In 2016, people will have observed both those favouring the UK continuing to be in the European Union and those favouring leaving the European Union, trying to set the agenda. In the USA politicians such as Donald Trump set the agenda on many issues during the presidential election.

Alienation

This is the term first used by Karl Marx that workers had lost control over the tasks they did, and over how their products were used.

Antisocial behaviour

Sociologists have always been interested in behaviour that is seen to affect other people unfavourably.

Attention is given to how young people can affect the rest of society.

Apartheid

Whilst apartheid means separate development, in practice in South Africa it meant that the white population were separated from the black population who had inferior facilities including poorer health care, education etc. This was the system used from the late 1940s to the early 1990s when President De Klerk voluntarily gave up the system and was replaced by the late Nelson Mandela. The system is of interest to sociologists because they can observe the effects of segregation. Whilst the system is mainly associated with South Africa many parts of the south of the USA had a similar system.

Ascribed status

This is a position which people reach that is often fixed at birth. In the United Kingdom, this could refer to hereditary peers or the Royal family. In the Hindu tradition, it could refer to the caste system.

Authority

This refers to the power people have within organisations based on agreement. Sociologists can observe this for example in democracies where people can vote out the government if sufficient people wish to do this.

Sociologists can also observe it in organisations such as the John Lewis partnership where employees have the right to make decisions about business policy.

B

Beanpole family

This refers to the different generations within the family where each generation has one or a very few members.

Birth rates

This is the number of people born to 1000 women of a particular age group. In the United Kingdom and elsewhere, it has reduced, partly because of contraception and partly because women have wanted to have children later in marriage or a relationship. In many poorer countries, however, it is much higher, partly because where there is no welfare state provision people wish to have children who will look after them in their old age.

Bourgeoisie

Karl Marx one of the best-known sociologists used this phrase to mean the ruling class in a capitalist society. He assumed that the bourgeoisie owning the means of production would be able to influence society for their own ends rather than for the benefit of all.

The term petit bourgeoisie has also been used to mean the lower middle class.

C

Capitalism

This is the economic system where individuals own land, labour and capital which they invest in order to make profits for themselves.

Causation

Sociologists have always been interested in what causes either individuals or societies as a whole to alter their behaviour. This could include external influences on societies, for example, in the 19th century, the Japanese mixing with other societies often for the first time. It could also include currently the ways in which different ethnic groups have influenced society. This could be sometimes comparatively trivial as with the phrase curry and chips to denote the influence of immigration from the Indian subcontinent on British diet.

Charisma

This is where top people use their magnetism to persuade people to carry out certain actions.

In the United Kingdom Richard Branson who formed the Virgin group of companies is often described as charismatic.

Chivalry effect

Some sociologists have suggested that one of the reasons why fewer women are in jail or are convicted for criminal offences is that magistrates or judges are influenced by chivalry so that they impose lighter sentences or do not convict people.

More unusually, it applies to older people being thought of as unlikely to commit certain crimes so therefore they will be given the benefit of the doubt whereas others would not be.

Citizens

Citizens of the state have both legal rights, e.g. to be treated equally before the law irrespective of their income or background, and responsibilities e.g. to obey the laws of the particular state.

Citizens

These are members of a country who have the legal rights under the law of that country to be treated equally. In the European Union, membership might also confer both rights and responsibilities.

Citizenship

In the UK, this would usually include people born to UK parents but it can be acquired in the UK by undertaking a citizenship test as well as fulfilling certain other criteria.

Citizen test

In order to become a citizen of the United Kingdom, migrants must now pass a Citizenship test.

Civil partnership

This can apply to two members of the same sex entering into a contract in the UK that gives similar rights to those in a marriage.

In the United Kingdom, two people of the same sex can now have a legally recognised marriage.

Class

Sociologists have always been interested in class and how it affects society as a whole. They are also interested in how far people particularly in the lower social classes can get equal opportunity of education, access to good housing, and being able to live in a pleasant environment rather than one that is heavily polluted.

Classless society

This refers to a society where there are different social classes. Some of the early sociologists suggested that in hunter-gatherer society there were no social classes.

The clean air act 1957

In the UK, this came into force after a series of smogs killed many people (one estimate was around 2000 people) particularly in the London area in December 1952. The term smog refers to a mixture of smoke and fog. In 1957, coal fires were used for heating in homes, shops and industrial premises. Steam trains also dominated the railway system. Some sociologists, particularly from the eco-sociological school, suggest we need a similar act now, as road vehicle pollution kills around 30,000 people per year in the UK.

Climate change

Most eco-feminists regard this as the main challenge to human society. Sharon Beder of the University of Wollongong has shown how the fuel companies have often distorted information about climate change. The Governor of the Bank of England has also described it as a major threat to the world economy.

Coercion

This is where people obey other people because of threats. We can see extreme examples of this with Isis (so-called Islamic state) are in a number of different countries. We can see less extreme examples, in schools where there may be a threat of exclusion if pupils do not conform to the rules laid down by the head teacher.

Cohabitation

This is where people have sexual relationships outside either marriage or a civil partnership. It has become increasingly common in the UK partly because of secularisation and less concern with religious observance.

This is where people live with another partner having sexual relationships where they are not either husband-and-wife or in a civil partnership.

Collective action

This is where large groups assembled in a particular place, such as in Trafalgar Square in central London may demonstrate their opposition or approval of austerity measures or their views about wars such as that against Iraq in 2003. In 2016, people demonstrated about austerity cuts.

Command economies

This is the system where the government makes the major decisions about the allocation of land, labour and capital. Until the late 1980s most of Eastern Europe was under the control of the Soviet Union, which allocated resources in this way. Cuba is still an example of a command economy but it is changing rapidly. An example of this was the visit by President Obama of the USA who became the first serving president since 1928 to visit the country in 2016.

North Korea is an extreme example of a command economy. Not only does the state make nearly all of the major decisions, but also any dissent is punished extremely harshly.

Communications

Communications use information to be transmitted from one group to another. This can be either verbal or non-verbal, and in the 21st century is rapidly being altered by the digital revolution. The use of mobile phones to transmit photos means it is often easy for people to get information very quickly over vast distances.

Communism

Karl Marx used the phrases socialism and communism interchangeably. The term communism usually refers however to the system such as in China where the state controlled decisions such as the number of children it allowed to be born in a family, which would usually be thought of as a private decision.

Communitarianism

This phrase originated in the USA and led to a movement with the same name. It has often been associated with the right wing Christian fundamentalists. Communitarians believe that there has been a breakdown of the community with continued movement toward excessive individualism and consumerism.

They would like people to be able to monitor other peoples' behaviour if these people fail to live up to the rest of the community's standards. Generally, they would also associate a lack of community with a decline in moral standards and the general loss of the traditional family system.

Comte

Auguste Comte (1798 -1857) is usually regarded as the founder of sociology as a discipline. He adopted a positivist approach, meaning that theories can be proved or disproved through relevant evidence.

Conflict approach

Karl Marx assumed that generally there would be conflict between the different classes. Whilst he assumed that the landowner class would oppress the proletariat, landowners and other organisations may also come into conflict, especially with large-scale infrastructure such as the proposed "high-speed two" line between London, Edinburgh and Glasgow.

Conflict theory

Karl Marx assumed that society as a whole is based on conflict between different classes. Some other sociologists suggest that major religions will form the major tensions in future conflicts.

Conformity

Sociologists have always been interested in the ways in which people either to conform to social norms because of their acceptance of the underlying values or sometimes because of sanctions. They will also be interested in why particular groups for example, teenagers might reject the norms of society. Currently there are debates in the UK about why some radical Muslims have rejected the underlying values of British society. There are also debates about why extreme right wing groups have taken part in violence.

Conglomerates

These are large companies with a range of different unrelated products and services.

Many of the largest conglomerates have a vast degree of power over society across nations. Examples of conglomerates include Nestlé the giant food firm.

Conglomerates would also include the giant media organisations that control television channels and the press.

Consensus approach

This is where people come together to try to find a solution to problems which is acceptable to all.

Consensus theory

This assumes that people can find ways of accommodating people with different backgrounds whether class or religion so that harmony can usually prevail. In the UK, this is sometimes referred to as the John Lewis approach since that company is owned by its employees and many suggest this is why the company has flourished for a long period. Whilst the mass media concentrate on conflicts in businesses and other organisations, people are often satisfied at work and sociologists may be able to advise organisations on how to achieve this satisfaction.

Convergence theory

Convergence theory suggests that large organisations often pursue their own objectives, rather than in the public sector, the interests of the public or in the private sector the interests of the shareholders. Some people might suggest therefore that managers pursue their own interests within certain constraints, and that in practice large-scale organisations are often not accountable to anyone.

Corporate crimes

These are crimes by employees or managers of companies or other business organisations which affect society as a whole. Currently many social scientists are concerned by the frauds committed by these organisations. Hacking into people's computer data is common. In 2016 Yahoo reported that about 500 million of its accounts had been hacked into and it was assumed that this was an example of corporate crime.

Correlation

This is the statistical term measuring the extent of a relationship between one variable and another. A perfect correlation will have the number +1 or -1. It is rare to find the perfect co-relation, but sociologists have often been interested in the relationship between poverty and other factors such as unemployment, demographic, such as size of family level of education and so on. Sometimes it is obvious which factors cause another, for example, in ordinary life, we know that higher temperatures result in an ice cream melting. Sometimes we are not so certain, for example, does watching too much violence on television, lead to violence in real life or does violence in real life, lead to people wanting to watch more violence on television.

The created environment

This refers to the infrastructure and other buildings created by human beings. This would include roads, railways, ports and airports, which often have a considerable impact upon the people around them. It would also include offices, factories, as well, as homes. In 2016 the current UK government wishes to expand transport and other infrastructure in order to create more jobs.

Crimes

These are illegal acts. They can range from minor offences such as parking too long in a particular area to crimes against humanity involving large-scale massacres of individuals.

Cultural deprivation

This is the phrase often used about children who may not receive adequate support from their parents, making it difficult for the children to do well at school.

There has recently been more concern expressed by sociologists about children in care, who receive less support up to the age of 18 and often none provision after the age of 18.

Culture

This may be defined as the collection of norms affecting a particular society. Sociologists will be interested in how cultures develop, partly from mixing with people from other cultures. There are occasionally cultures, especially in very mountainous country or other inaccessible places where people will not have mixed.

D

Data

Sociologists are interested in data since they frequently want to test different hypotheses to look at the effects of changing circumstances. This could include the development of e-commerce and the effects it has on potential workers as well as on people who do not have access to the Internet. Supermarkets and other organisations generate considerable volumes of data about their customers. Census data such as that from 2011 is an important source of information for many sociologists.

Demerit goods and services

These are goods or services, which are regarded as bad by the government or other bodies. This would include tobacco, which in the UK currently kills around 100,000 people per year. The Labour government in 2007 restricted smoking in public places including shops, offices and factories. Alcohol has often been regarded as a demerit good and during the prohibition era in the USA sales of alcohol were banned, completely. Many drugs, including cannabis are banned, but a large minority of people have taken them. Even legal demerit goods are often taxed considerably to reduce their consumption. The Danish government has imposed a tax on fatty food. In the UK, the Conservative government has come under pressure to impose similar taxes because of the problems of obesity.

Division of labour

Sociologists, since the time of Karl Marx have been interested in the division of labour and its effect on society. Whilst it has given higher standards of living, it also imposes threats to specialist employees if circumstances change. In the United Kingdom, railway signalmen and railway drivers are concerned about changes in technology. These particular groups, whilst highly skilled do not have transferable skills. Similarly, there are concerns across Europe about the decline in demand for steel and how this could affect people with skills in that industry. Apart from the problems of unemployment, some people are concerned that the extreme division of labour may lead to people not having rounded views.

Durkheim, Emile

One of the best known of the early sociologists, Durkheim is famous for assessing different rates of suicide across different cultures in his book suicide published in 1897. His analysis has however been criticised, since in countries with a strong Roman Catholic background suicide is regarded as a sin and therefore coroners and others may be reluctant to assess suicide as the cause of death.

He also wrote a book called the Division of Labour in Society, which was published in 1893.

E

The economy

Modern societies often judge their success or otherwise by the amount of production which people can use within society.

Many economists wrongly suggest that gross domestic product or gross national product per head is a measure of economic welfare without looking at vast amount of waste in many economies. For example, about one third of all the food in UK supermarket chains is wasted. Similarly, it would be possible through better insulation methods and greater fuel efficiency to reduce the volume of fuel being used without affecting people's welfare.

Education

Education has been studied by sociologists partly because of the impact it has on both incomes as well as status. The raising of the school leaving age to 18 in the United Kingdom as well as tuition fees for university students in England and Wales will also have attracted sociologist's attention. There are many different sociological views about how society can knit together so that harmony is the norm.

F

Feminists

Feminists have been concerned about the lack of progress made in many fields such as the quality of opportunity to obtain the highest positions in the law, politics or largest firms. As with other views, there are a wide number of different approaches by feminists, including black feminism, eco-feminism, radical feminism and liberal feminism.

Fertility

This is the average number of children born to women in the childbearing age. This has often been understood to be women between 15 and 44 but with IVF treatments becoming more common the upper range could become more extended. In April 2016, there was considerable publicity about the oldest woman ever to have triplets.

Folk Devils

Sociologists such as Cohen have looked at groups such as the mods and rockers in the 1970s that were regarded as a threat to society's norms. In 2016, there has been concern that all football fans can be regarded as potential thugs.

Formal social control

Many different agencies exercise control over our behaviour. This includes the police force, judges and magistrates, and prisons.

Functionalist approach

Sociologists belonging to this school of thought have often looked at the ways in which societies function by analogy with machines and the human body so that all the functions have to be working smoothly if society is to flourish.

G

Gender

Sociologists have often been interested in the ways that men and women have been treated sometimes at an early age and how this affects society as a whole.

Gender roles

These are the ways societies assign different roles to men and women.
In the UK and USA, this has often taken a traditional form so that women have been responsible for childcare whilst men have been the wage earners. This is changing rapidly partly because of the changing nature of jobs.

Geographical mobility

This refers to people moving sometimes within a country as for example more people moving to the London area. It can also refer to international migration, which hit the headlines in 2016.

Globalisation

This has become much more important, with generally freer trade between developed nations. In 2016, there were many discussions about the effect of reductions in demand for steel and the effects on economies, including the UK. In the USA presidential election in 2016, Pres Donald Trump argued strongly against globalisation which caused unemployment to many blue collar workers in the USA.

Gross domestic product

This is the total production within a country. It is often assumed wrongly that the higher the gross domestic product the higher is the welfare of the inhabitants. However, this ignores wasteful competition, when, for example, goods, especially food are transported long distances from where they are produced to shops and supermarkets near where they first came from.

Apart from this criticism is usually advisable, when looking at a time series to look at gross domestic product per head since if the population grows rapidly for whatever reason, more goods and services would be necessary to maintain the same standard of living.

H

Hidden curriculum

Whilst the phrase "hidden curriculum" is used by Bowles and Gintis it could be argued that Karl Marx thought that there were many features of teaching within the United Kingdom at the time he was writing which meant that school was being used to indoctrinate people into the world of work to which they would later belong.

One of these was that orders from above are obeyed and students quickly learn about the hierarchy within the school even if it is not officially stated. Educational prospectuses and websites will also set out the hierarchy, and students will soon learn, even at an early age, who is important. This can be seen as a prelude to work.

Students may see the effects of the hierarchy particularly at speech days, school assemblies and parents' days.

Ideas such as having to wait for teachers before the students are allowed to enter classrooms would be part of the idea of being subservient to teachers. They will also have noticed that the teachers in turn will often let the head teacher have priority in the classroom if he or she enters.

Hierarchy

Sociologists have looked at the ways in which power occurs within a society. In feudal societies for example, the King or Queen had immense power whilst the "serfs and villeins" had very little power. In 2016, Sir Philip Green came under scrutiny when 11,000 people faced redundancies from the collapse of BHS.

In business organisations, chief executives may have considerable power whilst people on the shop floor may simply be wage slaves especially in countries where there is nothing to prevent this.

Household

This could be one person but could also include several people who share at least one meal a day or possibly share facilities such as a living area including a bathroom or toilet.

Hypothesis

Sociologists will form hypotheses such as what is the link between educational attainments and wages. They will wish to have hypotheses that can be tested, often using quantitative methods.

I

Identity

People may identify themselves in a variety of different ways. This could be by a particular area with which they associate. Many sociologists noted with the Scottish referendum on independence in 2014 that some people identified themselves as Scottish rather than British. Similarly, in the 2016 referendum on the United Kingdom leaving or staying in the European Union some people identify themselves as solely British whilst others identify themselves as European.

Ideology

These are ideas or beliefs, which individuals or groups hold. They often serve the interests of the dominant class, and in 2016, the leaked Panama papers showed how large scale corporations and others could avoid paying corporation tax, etc. whilst telling poorer people that they should pay their own taxes.

Imperialism

This often refers to the 19th century when many European powers, including the United Kingdom, France, Belgium, the Netherlands, established their rule over many parts of the world, especially Africa.

Incomes

Sociologists have been interested in incomes of individuals and households and the ways in which it affects people's behaviour as consumers and workers. Sociologists will often be interested in disposable incomes. This is sometimes referred to as take-home pay.

Infant mortality rates

This is the number of children under a certain age, sometimes 1 or 5 years old, who die per 1000 births. Infant mortality rates have fallen rapidly in countries such as the United Kingdom. There are still, however, considerable differences between these rates in different social classes.

Informal social control

Sociologists have often been interested in the ways that people are controlled in their behaviour by the wish to gain respect from other groups even if they have no formal control.

J

Joint conjugal roles

This is where men and women share tasks equally, rather than women carrying out an unfair proportion of the tasks. Whilst women now outnumber men in the total labour market in the United Kingdom, Ann Oakley a well-known sociologist suggests that women often do far more of the total hours worked in the week than men do.

K

Kinship

This is the relationship between individuals, which can occur through marriage and the family. Whilst in the UK and USA there may be few obligations outside a small number of people in many other cultures kinship can extend much further.

L

Life expectancy

This can refer to the number of years that males or females can expect to live. It has increased considerably from the 19th century to today in countries such as the United Kingdom. Women generally live longer than men for reasons which are not very clear. Sociologists will also be interested in the number of years that people expect to live from retirement age since pensioners are often among the poorer sections of society.

M

Maslow's hierarchy of needs

Whilst this is not usually regarded as a sociological term, it is implicit in much of their writing and thinking since it looks at what people's aspirations are. It shows that at the bottom there is concern about physiological needs and at the top self actualisation. For more details see David Spurling's, John Spurling's, James Gachihi's and Simon Cruikshank's book the principles of business and management.

Mental health

Mental health problems are said to affect about 25% of the United Kingdom population, but it is rarely taken as seriously as physical health problems. In the United Kingdom, about 6000 people per year commit suicide. Suicide was studied extensively by Durkheim, one of the early sociologists.

Middle class

This refers to the group of people, generally white-collar workers, who are neither extremely rich nor poor. A former Conservative the late Prime Minister Harold Macmillan once said, "We are all middle class now."

Military rule

Whilst Western Europe since the end of the Second World War has usually had democracy, military rule, which means government by military leaders, has been common in many parts of the world, including South America as well, as Middle Eastern countries. Sociologists have been concerned about the ways in which British and American governments have helped to prop up military rules in many other countries.

Minority ethnic group

In the United Kingdom, this would include many people from the Indian subcontinent and many from the Eastern European countries.

Monotheism

This is the term used to describe a belief that there is one God. Christians, Muslims and Jews would subscribe to this belief.

N

Negative sanctions

This is where rules are enforced in a negative way by punishments. Sometimes this is referred to as stick methods rather than carrot methods.

New media

This refers to digital television as well as to the Internet. Sociologists are interested in new media since it can transform life partly because of the number of hours that many people are on the Internet and partly because it can widen the opportunities for people to be able to sell goods and services on a global basis. It also gives considerable power to those providing such services to get private information about its users. In 2016, there was considerable controversy about the ways that Intelligence Services wish to get information from the big organisations such as Apple. The Intelligence services claim that they need such information to counter terrorism. Other sociologists would suggest that having too much power in too few hands leads to a democratic deficit.

The New Right

The New Right have become more important since the 1980s and 1990s. In 2012 Sarah Palin stood as the vice-presidential candidate for the Republicans and was regarded as one of the New Right. In 2016 the Republican presidential candidate Donald Trump has been very much associated with the New Right and has now been elected president.

Norms

Sociologists have always been interested in the values underlying people's behaviour. This would extend to the ways that the British are expected to queue when waiting for a cinema or theatre performance. It would also apply to the ways in which people waiting for a doctor to see them would be expected to behave.

Nuclear family

The nuclear family has become much more common in the United Kingdom. It means a two-generation family with a mother or father, or both and a child or children. It does not necessarily mean that the father and mother are married since they could be cohabiting.

O

Obesity

Sociologists have been interested in this, partly because it is now one of the major factors affecting both lifespans and a number of serious illnesses including many cancers. Sociologists will be interested in how they can help people to avoid comfort eating and in what ways they can reduce people's desire to eat either too much or too many unhealthy foods. Better labelling of foods showing the number of calories etc may help reduce this problem.

Official statistics

In the United Kingdom, these are often provided at government level by the office For National Statistics.

They are expected to give figures in an unbiased fashion as possible. This has been particularly important at budget time and in the run-up to elections and referendum votes, such as the Scottish independence referendum of 2014 and the referendum about membership of the European Union in 2016.

Official statistics can also be provided by local authorities. Local authorities will keep statistics since they often wish to know and forecast the number of children who will be wishing to attend schools in the future. They will also need to forecast the number of homes and other buildings necessary for the community to thrive.

One child policy

This has been prevalent in communist China for a considerable period but was relaxed slightly from 2016. It is of interest to sociologists especially because the high economic growth rate of China will pose problems for climate change.

P

Patriarchy

This usually means the domination by men of women.
One of the main writers about patriarchy has been Sylvia Walby especially in her book "theorising patriarchy" published in 1989. [35]

Peer group

Sociologists have often studied the peer group, especially the younger generations. Peer group refers to people who have a similar status in society and Paul Willis in his book "learning to Labour "published in 1977 shows how white working-class boys in the 1970s West Midlands shared similar views about education.

Currently sociologists will be interested in the ways that young criminals will react with each other. Increasing levels of violence in British jails will also interest them,

Peer review

Conferences including videoconferences are often important for social scientists, including sociologists. Usually before articles or papers are presented, they will be assessed by experienced social scientists.

It is not however just social science papers need to be reviewed. Medical articles can also influence society very greatly as can major infrastructure developments and sociologists will be interested in the assumptions that people make.

An example of this will be the proposed "High-Speed Two" link between London, Edinburgh and Glasgow where the developers wish to take into account the likely reactions of stakeholders and how they can therefore improve the project without undue expense.

Political parties

in 2016, the Conservative Party, the Labour, the Scottish National Party, the Democratic Unionist Party, the Liberal Democrats, Sinn Féin, Plaid Cymru, the Social Democratic & Labour Party, the Ulster Unionist Party, the Green Party, and the UK Independence Party all held seats in the UK's House of Commons.

Political parties will put forward policies on a range of different issues such as whether to leave the European Union or to stay in it. In 2016, there were debates within the parties and between them about the expense involved in maintaining Trident, as well as how to deal with the migration problem.

Polytheism

This is the term used to denote a belief in many gods rather than one.

Population (of an area)

Social scientists, including sociologists have always been interested, not merely in the total population of the country but the demography within it.

This is because an ageing population will have different demands to those of the younger generation, as well as the effects on the Labour market.

Population of a sample

This refers to the particular population the sociologists wish to study. In 2016, concerns about the increasing extent of dementia prompted the government to ask medical practices to look at all the population over 40 years old.

Sociologists may be able to advise government on how to deal with some of the issues since, for example, it is correlated with loneliness.

Positive sanctions

This is where people are rewarded for behaviour considered acceptable to the people in charge. This could include praise at organisational meetings. It could also include financial rewards such as payments in kind.

A travel company for example might offer people free accommodation, and similarly a transport company might offer free travel on some journeys.

Poverty

Sociologists often distinguish between absolute poverty where people's incomes are below that necessary to survive. We can see many examples of this in the Third World; sociologists have coined the phrase the fourth world to mean people such as the homeless in the United Kingdom, where the life expectancy is often below that of people in the Third World. Sociologists have also written about relative poverty, for example being able to afford access to broadband.

Poverty trap

Sociologists have sometimes used this phrase to mean people where, because of the taxation and benefits system, an increase in pay does not leave them any better off.

Pressure groups

These groups try to persuade governments to accept a particular point of view about different measures. Pressure groups can be altruistic as in the case of Oxfam, Christian aid, or can try to influence the government for selfish reasons, such as the fuel lobby, resisting attempts to reduce pollution.

Similarly, some groups have been set up to try to prevent restrictions on tobacco use, even though Prof Richard Doll had discovered the correlation between smoking and health in 1950.

Primary research methods

These are common in sociology, where secondary research is not possible. This is where sociologists and others collect data sometimes through observation of small or large groups, and sometimes through surveys.

Proletariat

This term, used by Karl Marx and other sociologists, refers to the people who are oppressed in a capitalist society.

Public schools

In the United Kingdom, about 7% of the relevant age cohort goes to public schools. The best-known boys' public schools are Eton and Harrow. At the beginning of 2016, David Cameron, the then Prime Minister, George Osborne, the Chancellor of the Exchequer, and Boris Johnson, the former Mayor of London and Conservative Cabinet Minster were all educated at Eton.

Q

Qualitative data

This data is presented, either in words or with pictures. This may occur, for example with in depth surveys about individuals, where we wish to find out the extent of influences.

Quantitative data

This is where sociologists present information, to show the extent of particular influences, social scientists will often present information in terms of graphs, or Excel using spreadsheets. It may show the extent of correlation.

Quota sampling

This is where sociologists investigate a number of people conforming to the population they wish to question. For example, they might want to interview 400 people who are over the age of 65 and are householders.

R

Reconstituted family

This is a family where there are stepchildren, so that one or other of the current partners have had a child or sometimes several children from a previous relationship.

Reliability

This is important to sociologists, as they often wish to test whether the findings from surveys are consistent with previous data.

Replication

Social scientists want to look at research methods, including questionnaires, that can be repeated by other researchers, so that reliability can be established

Representative democracy

In the United Kingdom, voters are represented by a number of different representatives, including district councillors, county councillors, MPs and MEPs who make decisions on behalf of the people they represent

Restricted code

Some sociologists have used the phrase "restricted code" to mean language used by the working class with limited vocabulary which makes it difficult for them to communicate with teachers, teaching assistants and other education officials. It may also make working class parents less able to fill in forms and thus can add to their poverty.

Revolution

This refers to the overthrow of regimes by large-scale social movements, usually involving force. In the 18th century, The French revolution, 1789 had considerable effect on many other nations. In the 20th century, Sociologists were often interested in the Russian revolution of 1917 when the Tsar of Russia was overthrown and it became a Communist country instead. The Iranian revolution 1979 when the former Shah was overthrown was important partly because of the effects on the oil industry and partly because it changed the political framework in the Middle East.

Roles

Sociologists are interested in what is expected of people who have a particular role; this could include parents, NHS staff as well as managers.

S

Sample

This is the number and type of people who are being investigated for research purposes

Scapegoat

This is a group or individual who are blamed for societies problems. In the 1930s, the Nazis blamed the Jews for the majority of their problems. Some now use similar rhetoric regarding migrants from a number of different countries.

School ethos

Sociologists have been interested in the ways that schools vary on the approach towards behaviour, allowing students to choose school councils or not allowing them any say at all.

Schools of thought

There are many different schools of thought in sociology, including Marxism, functionalism, and feminism and the New Right.

Science

Physical sciences mean where we study systematically what happens in the physical world. The idea in science is that we can put forward hypotheses, which can then be tested or rejected according to the evidence. There is however a danger that science can be used not only for good purposes, such as studying causes of cancer and therefore helping to reduce the incidence, but as in Nazi Germany in the 1930s to find more efficient ways of killing people.

Secondary sources of information

Sociologists may use information that has already been published, including data, such as the 2011 census data in the United Kingdom.

Secularisation

This is the term used to denote decline in observation of religion in countries such as United Kingdom.

Selective education

In the United Kingdom, about 7% of the total school population are educated in public schools where parents often pay substantial school fees. In areas, such as Kent, students are selected based on their performance in the 11+ test.

Self-consciousness

In ordinary life, we usually use the phrase to mean shyness. Social scientists, including sociologists are interested in self-consciousness, partly because extreme self-consciousness may affect people's ability to communicate, but also partly because self-consciousness affects the processes by which children learn.

Self-fulfilling prophecy

This may occur through labelling people as either very good or very bad so then the people's performance whether at work or in education reflects this assessment.

Sexism

This refers to discrimination based on gender. In the United Kingdom, discrimination with minor exceptions such as where personal decency could be at risk is prohibited. However, in the United Kingdom women are currently underrepresented in Parliament, in top management positions at major firms, and in schools. The Sex Discrimination Act 1975 and later legislation including The Equality act 2010 aim to prevent discrimination against men or women.

Social cohesion

This is where different people as well as groups have common norms that bind them together rather than dividing them. Areas such as Northern Ireland and Syria suffer where there is little social cohesion.

Social exclusion

This is where people either are or perceive themselves to be excluded from the main facets of society such as cultural norms or political life.

Social mobility

Currently there are concerns that many groups in society cannot move up a layer because of lack of education or discrimination. There can be social mobility downwards especially when large-scale unemployment occurs in a particular area.

Stakeholders

This is usually regarded as a business term, and looks at the impact of a project on those who are affected by it. This could include for example, employees, managers, customers, suppliers, rivals as well, as people living in the neighbourhood of the project. An example of this is what happens to the stakeholders, if a steel mill is shut in the northeast of England to all these different groups. It is a useful method of assessing arguments for and against governments at a variety of levels as well as trade unions when trying to assess the advantages and disadvantages of particular course of action.

Stereotype

This is where people have a fixed of view of other groups such as the Roma who often used to be called gypsies or hoodies or people of a different religion. Stereotyping can also apply to age groups, with the concept that young people are automatically irresponsible, or older people will find it difficult to adapt to changing circumstances.

Strata

Sociologists have suggested that we have Strata in some societies with the ruling classes such as the monarchy being firmly entrenched, whilst other people have very little if any status at all.

Streaming

This is where in schools or sometimes colleges students are first grouped according to their general ability. They then retain this group across all the subjects they study. Many teachers and lecturers would criticise this system, since for example one person may be very good at English but very poor at mathematics.

Therefore, the student may not be stretched while studying English but may feel very frustrated when faced with mathematical concepts that seem beyond their grasp.

Subcultures

This is a group that differs from the mainstream culture in some way. For example, in the USA the predominant stream has often been said to be the Wasps (white Anglo-Saxon Protestants) so that the Hispanics i.e. those of Spanish origin can be regarded as a subculture.

Symmetrical family

This phrase, used by the late Lord Peter Willmott and Michael Young, denotes a family where duties are shared fairly by the different members.

T

Terrorism

Terrorism has caused many deaths in countries such as Syria, Iraq and other parts of the Middle East especially since the so-called Arab spring in 2012. Sociologists will be interested in why people get involved in acts of terrorism and how terrorists choose their targets. In 2016, there has been considerable emphasis on trying to prevent people from the UK and other countries from joining the jihadists in Syria and other countries.

U

Underemployment

This can apply in traditional societies where people often work as a family group and where there are for example bad harvests people will have very little to do.

Unemployment

The early sociologists were often interested in this because it often rose after major wars such as the Napoleonic wars where soldiers and sailors being discharged could not find work. More recently following the credit crunch 2008 onwards unemployment rose considerably in many countries causing major problems to society as a whole.

Urban ecology

Sociologists would suggest that people are affected by plants and animals around them, not just because of climate change, but because they influence people's behaviour.

V

Victim surveys

This is one of the ways of trying to measure crime in the United Kingdom. It may also help in trying to assess the mental stress as well as physical costs that occur to victims of crime. For example, people may not be able to go back to work if they have faced harassment on their way to or from work or whilst at work.

W

Welfare dependency

This is a phrase used by the current Conservative government but has been used by sociologists to denote people often from several generations who have become over reliant on the State providing welfare rather than looking for jobs to overcome the problems.

White-collar crimes

This usually refers to people in the upper echelons of society who commit crimes. There has been recent concern about major frauds carried out at a high level by the financial industry, and currently the banks are still suffering from problems because of this.

X

Xenophobia

This refers to extreme hatred of people of other races. The most extreme examples where during the third Reich in Nazi Germany and led to the Holocaust. More recently, we have seen extreme examples in Rwanda where average life expectancy fell to 20 during the civil war.

Y

Youth culture

Youth culture is sometimes described as a subculture. This is because it is assumed that teenagers have different characteristics to the rest of society. However, most sociologists would suggest that this depends very much upon the particular country. In many poorer countries, the teenagers will be part of the working population with very little money and resources.

Z

Zero tolerance

This phrase has sometimes been used when there have been riots or antisocial behaviour. It is often associated with the New Right on the assumption that offenders are rational and will weigh up the chances of being caught and will therefore be deterred from a particular offence. Critics however will suggest that zero tolerance has not been applied to more serious offences, such as fraud or selling arms to unsavoury regimes, which cause far more problems than drunken behaviour.

---

35 Sylvia Walby, *Theorizing Patriarchy* (Oxford: Blackwell, 1990) ISBN 978-0-631-14769-5

Chapter 20   How to use this book to get the best possible marks in GCSE sociology or equivalent exams

It is always helpful to check the latest syllabus to ensure that you know how long the examination lasts and therefore how long you have to answer particular questions or sections within the questions.

It is wise, even at an early stage, to check how much you can write legibly within the time given. It is also worthwhile checking that you understand the keywords that are expected in the answer. Examination boards such as AQA and OCR can provide you with information via their website about past examination papers and perhaps more importantly with their marking schemes.

Read a good quality newspaper such as The Times, The Guardian, The i, or The Daily Telegraph. Whether you read it in the paper format or in a downloadable format is unimportant. It is worthwhile however, making a note of events that are likely to alter society's norms and have an impact upon their objectives.

This means that you can have an idea of major changes in society.

If you look at the chapter in the book covering these topics, then you can add context to that material. For example, you can scrutinise the ways in which a major election is dealt with by the mass media.

This should help to motivate you to realise that, whilst your main objective may be simply to pass the examination, if you understand the major events you are no longer studying in a vacuum.

When looking at past examination papers it is often helpful to think what alternative questions could have been asked using the same information. Going laboriously only through the past examination questions is not always helpful since examination boards have commented that often students have not read the questions carefully but have put down answers to questions which they expected to turn up. Looking at marking schemes therefore and trying to see what alternative questions could have been asked is usually very helpful. The self-examination questions in the book are there, to guide you in this direction.

How the examination is marked

Examinations are not marked solely on your knowledge of the subject but also on your analysis, application and evaluation of the topic discussed.

Many students find it difficult to get a balance when they are answering the question where they have strong views in one direction. It is therefore often helpful to look at opposing views to those that you hold. You are entitled to your own value judgements in the examination but it is important to look at the evidence for and against particular measures. If you can find a friend who has completely different views to yours, but where neither of you will become too stressed when arguing, this is often very helpful.

Using role-play and introspective reasoning

Using role-play may well be helpful; imagining how different individuals or groups would react to particular events can be easy. The introspective approach can be used, i.e. "What would I do in these circumstances?" Psychologists often use the phrase fight or flight to mean that we can sometimes pretend we have not seen something is happening or sometimes we will immediately try to stop what is happening. The book gives many examples of the dilemmas people face. You may be able to use this as a basis for new information, which you can acquire from television programmes etc.

Some schools and colleges have additional classes before the examinations to help their students and it is often advisable to go to them. Feedback not just from the teacher but also from other students is helpful. Being able to contribute to discussions having read the book will help both you and other students.

You need to know your own pattern of learning; some people find it helpful to revise with others so that they can discuss ideas. Other people prefer to study on their own.

Trying to cram all the ideas in at the last moment is rarely a good idea!

Chapter 21   Index

A

Alcohol 184
Association 177
Asthana, Anushka 29

B

Beder, Sharon 189
Blair, Tony 175
Boeing 180
boomerang generation 52, 64, 199
Bovine Spongiform Encephalopathy (BSE) 175
British Broadcasting Corporation (BBC) 182

C

Cable, Sir Vince 79
Cameron, David (b 1966) 28, 73, 96, 102, 137, 192, 232
changing parent-child relationships 52
Chartered Institute of Logistics and Transport 186
Christian Aid 121, 169
Comecon 177
Computers 181
consensus 1, 2, 140, 215
Culture 183, 185

D

Darwin, Charles 250
Darwin, Charles (1809-82) 24
Davis, Nicola 13
Democratic Unionist Party (DUP) 97, 230
Dowler, Millie (1988-2002) 9
Drugs 176
Dubs, Alfred, Baron Dubs (b 1932) 27
Durkheim, Emile 190

E

education
    further 15, 20, 41, 197
    higher 15, 23, 33, 52, 198, 199, 220
    preschool 14, 134
    primary 14, 19, 101, 126
    secondary 14, 15, 19, 20, 23, 32, 33, 41, 126, 248
ethical issue 7, 8, 197

F

Fabes, Stephen 12, 13
feminism 1, 31, 91, 220, 235
Free Trade 172
Friends of the Earth 190
functionalism 1, 149, 235
further education 15, 20, 41, 197

G

Galton, Sir Francis (1822-1911) 24
Gates, Bill 173
Genetically Modified (GM) Crops 190
Giddens, Anthony, Baron Giddens (b 1938) 29, 30, 45, 85, 93, 182, 188, 193
Globalisation 167, 170, 172, 182, 192, 193
Global Warming 169
Goethe, Johann 184
Gove, Michael (b 1967) 27
Green, Damian Howard (b 1956) 27

H

hacking 9, 85, 93, 137, 194, 195, 216
halo effect 10
Hawthorne experiment 10
Heritage Foundation 189
higher education 15, 23, 33, 52, 198, 199, 220
Hillsborough disaster (1989) 12, 85
Hilton, James (1900-54) 23, 249
Hoxha, Enver 177
Hughes, Thomas (1822-96) 21, 23
hypothesis 3, 25, 36, 133, 196, 218, 223, 235

I

International Maritime Organisation 187
Investigatory Powers Bill 9, 192

K

Karadžić, Radovan (b 1945) 24
Khrushchev, Nikita 176

L

longitudinal studies 8, 21, 32, 63, 66, 196

M

Marshall Aid 178
Marxism 1, 235
Marx, Karl 68, 73, 106, 117, 125, 171, 173, 208, 209, 214, 215, 218, 222, 232
McDonalds 183
Measuring National Well-being 11, 86, 132
Merkel, Angela 192
Military Service Act 78

N

Nestlé 181

O

Oakley, Ann (b 1944) 30, 36, 225
Orde, Sir Hugh (b 1958) 27

P

patriarchal society 2, 89
Perlmutter, Amos 188
Pilger, John 170
pilot study 3, 4, 13
Plaid Cymru 97, 230
Poverty 176
preschool education 14, 134
Presley, Elvis (1935-77) 26
primary data 3, 7, 11, 65, 232
primary education 14, 19, 101, 126
Procter & Gamble 182

Q

Qatar 187
qualitative methods 9, 11, 112, 233

quantitative methods 11, 132, 134, 223, 233
Quinn, Ben 11, 13

R

Raising of the school leaving age (ROSLA) 15, 22, 52, 73, 219
random sampling 4, 5, 6, 197
Rashid, Ahmed 171
reliability issue 7, 9, 233, 234
representativeness issue 7, 9, 10, 13, 63, 130
Ritzer, George 183
Rowntree, Henry Isaac 181
Rural Areas 185

S

sampling 4, 5, 6
    random 4, 5, 6, 197
    snowball 4, 6, 7
    stratified 4, 6
    systematic 4, 7
secondary data 3, 7, 11, 65, 232, 236
secondary education 14, 15, 19, 20, 23, 32, 33, 41, 126, 248
Shepherd, Jessica 23, 75
Slavery 76
Snoopers❷ Charter. *See* Investigatory Powers Bill
snowball sampling 4, 6, 7
Soros, George 168
Springfield, Dusty (1939-99) 26
stratified sampling 4, 6
systematic sampling 4, 7

T

Tobin, James 168
Trade Unions 78
Transnational Corporations 167, 188
Travis, Alan 12, 13

U

Unilever 182, 188

V

validity issue 7, 9, 10
Vasagar, Jeevan 23

W

Walby, Sylvia (b 1953) 30, 31, 32, 33, 34, 35, 36, 37, 38, 39, 40, 45, 134, 229, 252
Wallerstein, Immanuel 173, 177
Walmart 167
Weber, Max (1864-1920) 25, 29, 173
Winton, Sir Nicholas George, MBE (1909-2015) 27

Chapter 22　　　　　　　　　　　　　　Bibliography

Chapter 10 "1905" – Leon Trotsky (978-0394715155)

Chapter 14 "A Church by Daylight" – Leslie Paul (978-0225659795)

Chapter 3 "All Our Future: a Longitudinal Study of Secondary Education" – James William Bruce Douglas (978-0586035276)

Chapter 9 "Anatomy of Britain" – Anthony Sampson (978-0719565663)

Chapter 9 "Animal Farm" – George Orwell (978-0141182704)

Chapter 4 "Bury the Chains; Prophets and Rebels in the fight to free an Empire's slaves" – Adam Hochschild (978-0618619078)

Chapter 10 "Dude, where's my country?" – Michael Moore (978-0141013008)

Chapter 14 "Evangelising the Cults" – Ronald Enroth (978-0850092318)

Chapter 14 The poverty and justice bible (978-1585169733)

Chapter 5 Climbing the bookshelves (autobiography of Shirley Williams) (ISBN: 9781844084753)

Chapter 6 "Family and Kinship in East London" - Michael Young & Peter Willmott (978-0141189123)

Chapter 15 "Folk Devils and Moral Panics" – Stanley Cohen (978-0415610162)

Chapter 10 "For Marx" – Louis Althusser (978-1844670529)

Chapter 17 "Globalisation" - Malcolm Waters (978-0415238540)

Chapter 3 "Goodbye, Mr Chips" – James Hilton (978-0340043592)

Chapter 10 "History of the Russian Revolution" – Leon Trotsky (978-1931859455)

Chapter 10 "Honest to God" – John Robinson (978-0334047339)

Chapter 1 "Human Societies: Introduction to Sociology" – Geoffrey Hurd (978-0415039857)

Chapter 14 "I Am Malala: The Girl Who Stood Up for Education and Was Shot by the Taliban" Malala Yousafzai - (978-1780226583)

Chapter 8 "The Invisible hand" - Adam Smith (978-0141036816)

Chapter 3 "Learning to Labour" – Paul Willis (978-1857421705)

Chapter 10 "Long Walk to Freedom" – Nelson Mandela (978-0349106533)

Chapter 11 "McDonaldization of Society" - George Ritzer (978-1452226699)

Chapter 11 "Mind, Self and Society" – George Mead (978-0226516684)

Chapter 11 "Modern Authoritarianism: A Comparative Institutional Analysis" – Amos Perlmutter (978-0300026405)

Chapter 4 "New racism; Conservatives and the ideology of the tribe" – Martin Barker (978-0890934715)

Chapter 16, a "Not on the Label" – Felicity Lawrence (978-0241967829)

Chapter 2 "On Origin of Species" – Charles Darwin (978-0241967829)

Chapter 1 "Reading Capital" – Louis Althusser (978-1844673476)

Chapter 14 "Religion and the Rise of Capitalism" – Richard Tawney (978-0140200232)

Chapter 14 "Religious Trends" - Peter Brierley (978-1850782810)

Chapter 14 Rich Christians in an Age of Hunger: Moving from Affluence to Generosity" – Ron Sider (978-0849945304)

Chapter 14 "Sacred Longings: Ecofeminist Theology and Globalisation" – Mary C. Grey (978-0334029281)

Chapter 9 "Small Is Beautiful: A Study of Economics as If People Mattered" - Ernst Schumacher (978-0099225614)

Chapter 1 "Sociology Themes and Perspectives" - Michael Haralambos and Martin Holborn (978-0007498826)

Chapter 1 "Sociology" – Anthony Giddens (978-0745652931)

Chapter 6 Stronger Families and Communities – Unlocking the potential of relationships" Chris Sherwood and Janet Walker (http://www.relate.org.uk/policy-campaigns/publications/stronger-families-and-communities-unlocking-potential-relationships)

Chapter 15 "Suicide" – Émile Durkheim (978-1607966425)

Chapter 2 "System of Positive Polity" – (Auguste Comte https://archive.org/details/systemofpositive02comt)

Chapter 14 "Taliban: Militant Islam, Oil and Fundamentalism in Central Asia" – Ahmed Rashid (978-1848854468)

Chapter 2 "The Course in Positive Philosophy" – Auguste Comte (http://socserv2.mcmaster.ca/~econ/ugcm/3ll3/comte/Philosophy1.pdf)

Chapter 8 "The Division of Labour in Society" – Émile Durkheim (978-0333339817)

Chapter 14 "The Elementary Forms of Religious Life" – Émile Durkheim (978-0199540129)

Chapter 9 "The English: A Portrait of a People" – Jeremy Paxman (978-0141032955)

Chapter 7 "The Letters of Private Wheeler 1809 - 1828" - B.H Liddell Hart (978-0900075582)

Chapter 11 "The McDonaldization of Society" – Professor George Ritzer (978-1452226699)

Chapter 14 "The New Tide of Militarisation" – The Luton Quakers (http://www.quaker.org.uk/militarism)

Chapter 11 "The Open Society and It's Enemies" – Karl Popper (978-0415610216)

Chapter 11 "The Poverty of Historicism" – Karl Popper (978-0415278461)

Chapter 9 "The Prison Notebooks" – Antonio Gramsci (978-0231157551)

Chapter 15 "The Professional Thief" – Edwin Sutherland (978-0226780511)

Chapter 9 "The Rise of Meritocracy" – Lord Michael Young (978-1560007043)

Chapter 2 "The Rules of Sociological Method" – Émile Durkheim (978-1476749723)

Chapter 14 "The Satanic Verses" – Salmon Rushdie (978-0963270702)

Chapter 14 "A Sociology of English Religion" David Martin (978-0435825744)

Chapter 12 "The Spirit Level; Why Equality is Better for Everyone" – Richard G. Wilkinson and Kate Pickett (978-0241954294)

Chapter 9 "The State We're in: Why Britain Is in Crisis and How to Overcome It" – Will Hutton (978-0099366812)

Chapter 8 "The Wealth of Nations" – Adam Smith (978-0140432084)

Chapter 5 Walby, Sylvia. *Theorizing Patriarchy.* Oxford: Blackwell, 1990. ISBN 978-0-631-14769-5

Chapter 9 "Who Rules Britain?" – John Scott (978-0745605630)

chapter 12. The rise of meritocracy, Lord Michael Young (978-1560007043

chapter 12, the spirit level, why equality is better for everyone. Richard G Wilkinson and Kate Pickett IBSN number 978-0241954294

chapter 14. A sociology of English religion. David Martin, 978-043825744

the new tide of militarisation-the Luton, Quakers

rich Christians in an age of hunger; moving from affluence to generosity- Ron Sider 978-0849945304

Lightning Source UK Ltd.
Milton Keynes UK
UKOW02f2046191216
290410UK00001B/38/P